MW01273487

School Stories

The **funny** thing about music

ROBERT STORMS

ISBN: 978-1-4834-9530-9 (sc)
ISBN: 978-1-4834-9529-3 (e)

Lulu Publishing Services rev. date: 03/27/2018

To the teachers and administrators of the
Ferndale School District #502

Ferndale, Washington

Preface

I came to Ferndale, Washington, in 1962. I would teach band and choir for two of the district's schools: Alexander Junior High, a large school in Ferndale, and Custer Middle School, a very small school located seven miles north of Ferndale in the town of Custer. The schools were bitter sports rivals; however, their rivalry status changed when the two schools eventually combined into the new Vista Middle School. Overnight, the Custer bunch became Vista students, in the "big" city of Ferndale (pop. 3,000).

As the years went by, students in my middle school band classes dubbed me a storyteller. My stories were always told with the intention of providing some educational value to the students. For example, I would tell of a previous band's contest problems to instruct my current students on how to avoid the pitfalls and consequential contest ratings of those who had gone before. I had many requests for certain stories (okay two), because those stories had already been shared by parents and reflected on *their* years in my middle school band. Somehow, the fact that the students found the stories funny made it all worthwhile for me, because laughter is contagious. The lessons were thus delivered amid smiles rather than faces that reflected words of stern warning.

During the 1990s, George Hunsby wrote recollections of his days as a logger in early Whatcom County. He shared them through a weekly column in the Bellingham Herald. I loved it—new stories every week that took you back to the days when Whatcom County was young, and told by a storyteller who, despite his age, was very clear in his memories of past events. And he wrote very well. One day, I had a chance to chat with George for about half an hour while relaxing in the foyer of the Leopold Hotel in Bellingham, where he resided. He told me that his memoir column was just like snapshots of life. I learned George's intention was to write objectively, neither praising nor criticizing anyone, anywhere, in his stories. He told me that he was paid twenty-five dollars for each column he wrote.

"The money didn't add up very fast," he said. But he didn't care. His column was popular and people began collecting them.

My stories were patterned somewhat after George's columns. The difference is that I tried to entertain a bit, to keep the stories from being too much like documentaries and more like stories that a friend would tell you. I wrote a weekly column, gratis, and the stories were published in the Ferndale Record Journal during the space of a year, beginning in March of 2006. I was told by the newspaper editor that requests were often received for reprints of stories missed by folks on vacation. That was the first I had heard of people collecting my stories. Other people later told me that they were saving my stories as well. It occurred to me that a book could serve the needs of collectors and would also give me an archive of my stories. The editor made that suggestion. He did so to cut down on the number of reprints he had to make each month.

When the Ferndale Boys and Girls Club building was heavily damaged by fire in 2007, I wanted to offer help. The idea of publishing the book and donating the proceeds toward rebuilding the club or replacing equipment for the kids seemed a good answer. So, with the assistance of local businesses and the Ferndale Record Journal, the book was published and the club was significantly helped. From sales of the first edition, I raised four thousand dollars for the Ferndale Boys and Girls Club. The new club has been built and is the pride of Ferndale.

The first edition of *School Stories* was a charming, folksy accounting of life in a middle school band room, with a few field trips and parades thrown in for good measure. Here, I have revisited those tales and added a few new ones to the mix. This second edition of *School Stories* is a more comprehensive collection, containing a few recollections of events that occurred before my first teaching job and some that occurred after the close of my teaching career.

There are stories of classroom pranks, unusual situations, problems, and decisions that shaped the outcome of a teacher's not-so-typical day in a public school music department. Also, there are a few stories that display the nuances of teaching both in a small school and a much larger one as they compete against each other in sports and annual parade band competition.

Each story is unique. The reader will see the problem I encountered and may be surprised at my chosen path toward solving it. For example, what is a teacher to do for a student with no arms who wants to play in the band like the other kids? There are stories of victory, tears, unexpected joy, and the personal aspects of making music over the span of my career, both while teaching and in retirement.

While storytelling is fun for me, it's also entertaining for others to hear of past events and to look back and laugh a bit. This is especially true for the band parents and past band students of mine. The day-to-day humor in the stories can be best described in just a few words: middle school music students; expect the unexpected. It is my hope that you will enjoy the stories of my teaching career in Ferndale. It was the best job I've ever loved.

Contents

HIGH
TIDE
LOW

First Parade Competition

During my first year of teaching, my Cle Elum High School Marching Band was invited to march in the Ellensburg Rodeo Parade. I asked the students about their interest in participating, and after receiving an overwhelmingly positive response, I submitted our entry form for the band adjudication.

Because I was a first-year teacher, my students were always telling me "how it was" the year before. The band hadn't marched in any parades throughout the previous year, they were very supportive of the marching idea, and our month of marching preparation went smoothly. We were all excited about this new band venture.

Parade Day came and our band members lined up for the parade, waiting for the starting instructions. As we stood, dressed in the school colors of Cle Elum High School, I became aware of something unsettling to the students. A band student ran up to me and announced that I should come quickly, as there was a car driving through the middle of the band, bumping the band members out of line. I was in disbelief but followed the student to the back of the band. Indeed, a car with two young men was ever-so-slowly moving forward through the band. The students were reluctant to move (break ranks) and the car simply pushed them out of the way. When I saw the car nudge two students aside, I took charge.

"Hold it right there!" I shouted, approaching the vehicle. The students immediately broke ranks and crowded around the car, awaiting the conflict that seemed sure to happen.

The driver rolled down his window and tried to explain his actions. He was simply going home. The two men lived in the dorm at the end of the street and refused to take another route. The parade made no difference to the driver; nor did the "Do not enter" sign behind his car. He started forward and the students in front of his car quickly jumped out of the way.

"Stop!" I yelled.

"Who is going to stop me?"

"Get out of the car and leave it here until the parade moves out. It's almost starting time." I used my best authoritarian voice.

He continued to move forward.

So I yelled, "Get out of your car!"

He did.

My students and I watched as a college man, who appeared to be six foot eight, got out and faced me. He stood behind his car door and I was on the other side of it, gasping for air at his size.

The students groaned, "Whoa!" as he stood there. It was a comedy act. This super tall dude with an attitude—think Goliath, here—looked down at a short guy in a white uniform.

In his best bass voice the student said, "Are you going to stop me?"

The kids all laughed. I didn't.

After a moment of reflection on the matter, I yelled, "Cle Elum football players, come forward!"

The college student asked, "You seriously want me to beat up your football team?"

"No," I answered.

Then I pointed to the front of the intruding car and said to the football team, "Grab the front bumper!"

"Now lift!"

Everyone was surprised when the front of the car rose off the ground.

"Now push!"

The car went backwards, forcing Goliath back into his retreating car. The boys ran the car for some distance, out onto the adjacent ball field, and left it there. The band cheered as they came back to the parade line-up. We had won the battle without a fight, and the heroes of the story were the members of the high school football team. Fair enough. I certainly couldn't have done it alone. They had indeed saved the day. I only helped.

When the parade was over we went to the college football stadium, where our band was to march in and play the national anthem before a sizable college crowd and then receive our marching award. We had won first place! The kids were joyous. I was in disbelief but also very happy.

At the stadium, our band was instructed to muster on the sidelines facing the fifty-yard line and wait for the announcer to call us onto the field. With the band finally in place and set in sharp lines from the front to the back ranks, the stadium speakers introduced the band and called it to enter the field. The crowd cheered. The band didn't move. The crowd kept cheering.

The drum major had left his whistle on the bus and didn't know how to start, stop, or play the band without his whistle. The announcer tried again, but still the band didn't move. Everyone could see the poor drum major running around in the band, holding his gold-wrapped scepter with its shiny, bulbous end, doing . . . something.

In the stands, I was having a fit! "Why won't he start the band?" I wondered aloud.

After a third plea from the announcer, the band suddenly came to life with their cadence and marched out onto the football field. "The Star-Spangled Banner" never sounded so good to my ears, for I had begun to think I would never hear it that day.

Following the national anthem, the band stood and awaited their marching trophy. The announcer was very gracious and gave the band high praise for its marching acumen.

"So now, we are pleased to present you with the first-place trophy in the high school marching division. As the Cle Elum High School Marching Band was the only high school band in the parade this year, we hope that you will join us again next year to defend your win."

We received a mixture of applause and laughter after the announcement. Our band students were shocked to hear that they had faced no competition. I suspected it, because I didn't see any other schools there. I had theorized that it was a long parade and surely the hometown band, Ellensburg High School, would be there.

In the weeks following marching season, I heard little talk about defending our win. The following year, not a single student asked about going to Ellensburg to march in the Ellensburg Rodeo Parade, so it wasn't scheduled.

"Okay, we quit while we're winners. What's wrong with that?" I said to myself. "Nothing. And I won't need to face Goliath again, either."

Memorial Day Memories

Near the end of the school year, during my first year of teaching in Cle Elum, Washington, my high school band had been asked to play for a Memorial Day ceremony in nearby Roslyn. The graveyard there had a white picket fence all around it and the band was given a place to play inside the fence. The crowd stood around a small platform onto which several dignitaries were ready to go, many of them in uniforms decorated with way too many medals.

The band was to play "The Star-Spangled Banner" and our trumpet player was to play "Taps." We had also been asked to play a march or two before the ceremony started. While getting into position, the crowd pushed us back against the fence. Instead of being free to move around a little, we were kind of pressed in there. We played our marches and waited.

The ceremony began, and a fellow in a dark blue suit said that we needed to pray together. As he did the honors everyone was very quiet. He included a prayer of remembrance for all the men who died in war. At this point, a man somewhere behind the band (we were facing the podium) started reliving his war experiences. We could not see him but he was right behind us.

As the minister was giving the prayer, suddenly we heard a voice behind us yelling, "Look out, Tommy, he's got a machine gun! Get down! Everyone, get down!"

Of course, our band got down on the ground. We really thought someone behind us had a machine gun and they were going to kill us.

"Hurry, get in the foxhole!" And then we heard, "Oh no, not you, Tommy!" Then he started crying.

Eventually, while lying on the ground, (there were other people in front of us lying on the ground as well), we realized that this was just someone reliving an experience. So, we got up very slowly, feeling rather sheepish. Oh, yeah, we were still on the lookout for a guy with a machine gun, though, just in case.

They eventually led that gentleman away.

Later in the service, our trumpet player was asked to go off into the trees and play the echo for "Taps." My student Clay walked into the woods and out of sight. An elderly man, wearing a batch of medals on his uniform and his hat at a rakish angle, came forward with his bugle. He struggled to play the melody. Actually, he barely could play the instrument at all. After each shaky phrase the echo came back crystal clear from Clay, who played with a beautiful trumpet tone. It was supposed to be a very reverent moment, but it almost became a comedy act because we all realized the elderly man wasn't going to be able to hit the high note near the end of the call. As the gentleman approached the note, the students in the band began to laugh, and this was not a very good thing. He missed the high note, even after several tries. Of course, Clay had no trouble with that note and he played it beautifully.

When it was over, a man came over to us and thanked us deeply for being there and putting up with the unusual situations and promising us that next year things would be much better.

It was better. We never received an invitation the next year.

Goodbye, and Thanks

The school year had ended. I had completed two years of my first job as a music teacher, and I was packed and ready to leave Cle Elum. I would head for the city of Ferndale and the promise of a new teaching job as middle school band and choir director.

I couldn't leave. Someone had driven up behind me and blocked the driveway as I backed out. I wasn't sure who the person in the car was and I didn't recognize his car. I got out of my car to see what this was all about and was approaching the vehicle when the man's door finally opened and a small, elderly gentleman got out. With a smile on his face, he said, "You can't leave town yet!" I recognized the man as a member of the men's choir I had started at the Cle Elum Community Church two years before.

He had tears in his eyes. "You can't leave town yet!" he said again, and then he hugged me. I wondered just what this man I barely knew was so emotional about, so after he let go of me he began to tell me just why.

"You saved my life!" he said.

"I did?"

The man's name was Henry and he was a nearly invisible member of the Community Church Men's Choir, as he was so short. The choir sang and he sang. That's it. I tried to remember any conversation I had with him that might have been potentially life-saving, but I drew a blank. His head went back and forth—from my chest, in a hug, to arm's length—as he told me his tale. His tears flowed.

"You let me join the choir. I'm not a good singer. You let me sing anyway." I was still in the dark when he piped up, "I was supposed to die two years ago." His grip on me tightened when he said that. "The doctor said that if I didn't use my lungs more I would not last until that Christmas. My tests were all showing falling numbers. I'm just a quiet person, I guess, and I don't use my voice very much." As he spoke, his grip relaxed and he looked at the ground. "That's when I asked the doctor what to do, and he said join a speech class, get in a discussion group and join in, or join a choir and sing loud."

Okay, I got it. He had joined the choir to get his lungs working. Interesting.

The fact that I was leaving town was not the big issue here, I realized. He simply wanted to credit me with saving his life, when it was his own actions that had saved him. As a young man, I had to try to relate to him somehow. My intention was to try to think of a comforting word, but none came.

Henry looked at me . . . and kissed me! I asked him why the kiss.

"It's from my wife."

Custer's Bees

The week before school started in 1962, the principal informed me, "You have your choice of any of five empty classrooms." That was because Custer had just changed to a middle school format from being a junior high, and on top of that the enrollment was projected to be down in the coming school year. I told him that I wanted the largest room, as the band simply takes more space per pupil. He then showed me the science room, touting its spaciousness, built-in storage cabinets, and the fact that it was a good distance from the bees' nest.

"Bees' nest?"

"Yes, bees' nest. It's a big nest in the corner of the old gymnasium and it's not a problem, except for an occasional bee in the classroom," he said.

I told him that I liked the room and I was glad he told me about the bees as I was afraid of the critters. I moved into the new band room feeling safe from the bees at the other side of the building. Things went well for a good part of the fall term and I enjoyed the small-school atmosphere of Custer Middle School and its seventeen-piece band.

But on one bright and sunny morning, as I directed the band through some training exercises in the band book, I noticed my young trombone player in the back row, pumping his slide skyward and around him from side to side. Curious behavior, even for a trombone player. So, I stopped the music and asked the lad what he was doing with the extra-curricular movements with his slide. He told me there was a bee in the classroom and it had been circling his head so he decided to poke at it with his slide to fend it off.

You know, there are times in life when you say the right thing, but everything suddenly goes wrong, as if in response to your statement. This was one of those times.

My sage advice to the young man was, "If you just leave the bee alone, it won't bother you. Don't try to poke at it or hit it. Just remain still and it will go away." The words had no sooner passed my lips when the bee came directly at me! I froze. I mean, I was petrified. I stood there, still holding my directing baton and poised to start the music, as the class watched in stunned silence.

It seemed to me that the bee was trying to teach me a lesson: "So you're supposed to remain still eh? Let's see how you like me going around your head, smart guy."

As the insect circled, I had visions of the little darling (someone's honey) deciding to explore one of my ear canals. He hovered and then buzzed one chosen ear while the class held its breath. Was he going in? If he did, what should I do? Oh yeah, take my own advice. Me and my big mouth.

The little honeybee did its best to scare me into some defensive action, like swatting, shaking my head, or running like a madman for the door. I'm sure I disappointed the little bugger by my inaction.

Then it did something rather unexpected. The bee lit on the tip of my baton and proceeded to slowly walk down toward the handle. The giant, sucking sound that accompanied that move was the class gasping in unison. The bee went down my hand and into the cuff of my sweat-soaked shirt.

All I had to do was squeeze the shirt and the problem would be solved. But in so doing, I would be demonstrating what I told the students not to do, so I stood still, waiting for the sting that seemed sure to follow. Instead, the bee emerged and trekked up to the tip of the baton and flew off toward the windows. An obliging student opened a window and the episode ended as the bee escaped unharmed.

When I began to say something to the class, the students interrupted me by clapping. I guess it was a good lesson for all, as I have not been afraid of bees since that day.

BREAD BOX
UNLEA
I SCREAM
TONES

A Bees' Nest and a Smelly Old Baritone

While teaching at Custer during the early 1960s, I was told that some band paraphernalia had been found in the old gym and it was all going to the dump. The principal allowed me to grant last-minute reprieves on any items destined for dumping. When I saw the small collection of odds and ends, one thing stood out like a snowy owl in a bare tree. It was an old, gold-colored, baritone horn with the initials "J.S." scratched on the case. The instrument inside was a bad combination of ugly and smelly. The valves were stuck solid. I decided to grant it a reprieve despite its unsavory condition.

In 1968, Washington State music teachers had their own administrator, a state supervisor of music. To my surprise, the newly-appointed music supervisor turned out to be a friend of mine, Jim Sjolund. When I mentioned his name to some of the other teachers at Custer, I was informed that indeed, mister now-to-be state administrator had graduated from Custer back in the 1950s.

What great news I had to tell our students that day. One of our very own Custer band players of the past was now the head of all the music in the state of Washington. I was determined to not let this go unnoticed. As the fall concert was in preparation, I decided to incorporate a welcome home to one of our own during the concert.

In contact with Mr. Sjolund, I found out that he indeed remembered playing in the Custer band, and later in the Ferndale High School band, and was quite proud of the experience. He casually mentioned that his instrument of choice was the baritone horn. I asked him to be the guest of honor at our fall concert and he accepted. Then I asked him if he remembered his old instrument when he was at Custer. He replied that he did, but he thought that his instrument was dumped years ago.

"What color was it?" I asked.

"Gold, as I recall. Almost all the brass instruments were lacquered gold back then. It was an old horn when I began playing it."

Each day brought more excitement to the students as they anticipated the arrival of their guest of honor. Boys were asking about the baritone. I told them that I had a surprise for Mr. James Sjolund when he arrived. Banners were made, announcing, "Welcome Back, Mr. Sjolund!"

On concert day our guest arrived in time to visit the school classrooms and look the school over a bit. He was quite surprised to find band being taught in the science room. I told him about the huge bees' nest in the corner of the old gym and he just laughed.

"It was there while I was in school," he said. "The nest was in the same area as the band room and the instruments were stored right next to the nest in the same corner of the room." That is precisely where I had rescued his old baritone.

The Custer Daughters of Rebekah put on a nice dinner before the concert and the public was invited to help celebrate the return of a local boy that "made good." Jim did his best to entertain the crowd of fifty or so attendees with his stories of attending school in Custer and the wonderful education he received there. The folks welcomed him in style. Custer style.

That night, during the concert, I introduced our guest to a standing ovation by the crowd of attendees. He made a speech in which he told of his days performing on a gold baritone horn and playing concerts in the old gym. As he spoke two boys approached him from behind, carrying the old baritone horn case. When he turned around to see what everyone was gawking at, he broke into a wide smile and said, "That's mine!" And it was. We gave it to him.

Of course, it had been my job to clean the instrument up and fumigate the case, but it was all his from there on. His face was bright red as he laughingly accepted the gift. We had surprised him. The students cheered with glee as he opened the case, to see his old friend, and then nodded to the audience that it was his all right. He told me that he played it all through school, that he started on the trumpet and later switched to baritone and loved playing it.

"The valves look better now," he noted. Of course, they were stuck solid and got a laugh from everyone when he tried to push them down and got nowhere.

Local Singer to National Star

In 1962, I came to Ferndale from Cle Elum, where I taught way too many classes for one guy. I taught high school band, junior high band, elementary band (four schools), high school choir, girls' glee club, dance band, and pep band. The latter two classes were after school, and on the nights when I didn't work with those classes I repaired instruments or taught free music lessons to better my band program. I was a "band guy" but I also enjoyed teaching a couple of vocal classes with good success.

When I interviewed for the job in Ferndale, Al Carr noted my vocal experience and quickly signed me up for Alexander Junior High and Custer School. Custer's outgoing ninth-grade class had just been moved to Ferndale High School. At that time FHS was a three-year high school.

During my teaching day in Ferndale, I spent time in the morning team teaching with Al Carr and the orchestra teacher, Ethel Crook. Both were master teachers and loved by their students. They were my mentors and I was very fortunate to have them as such.

In his capacity as high school choir teacher, Al asked me to work with one of his sopranos, MaryAnn Bailey. He told me that she had a beautiful voice but tended to sing sharp. He asked me to work with her to fix the problem. Well, it was quite an experience for me to work one to one with a soprano who had such a voice. I made my recommendations for improvement and did a bit of follow-up and found that everybody was happy, and that was the end of my short tutelage gig.

Little did I know that years later the very same young lady would go on to sing at the Metropolitan Opera. She became a local star, much like our local pro football players, Michael Koenen and Jake Locker, and pro coach, Doug Pederson. (As a sidelight, I taught Michael drums at Vista Middle School, and he was the first-chair player!) After her graduation from Oberlin Music School, MaryAnn Bailey joined the Hawaii Opera Company. She stayed with the company for many years and eventually was enticed away to join the hottest show around at that time, the *Jim Nabors Show*. She was a regular on the show and stayed with it for many years.

About 1980, I received a call from MaryAnn from her home in Hawaii. She wanted to enlist my help in locating a pianist to accompany her in a concert for the home folks in Ferndale. MaryAnn was attempting to "give back" to the community in which she had lived during her formative years. I asked her what made her think to call me, and her answer surprised me. She said that she got her first vocal encouragement from Al Carr, but when Al couldn't help he said that Bob Storms could, because he was a high tenor and Al was a bass. She pointed out that I also had told the high school students, in the car on our way to Washington's All State Choir, that it was not nice to laugh at someone whose big, anxiously awaited thrill would be to ride on an escalator in Spokane (aka the Big City).

The arrangements for a concert were next to impossible. The high school auditorium was booked solid. There was no place to hold the event that wouldn't be too expensive, so in desperation, she booked herself into a sports bar/restaurant in Ferndale's Pioneer Square. The management cleared the bandstand, brought in a piano and a microphone, and turned the place into Ferndale's very own one-night-only Opera Bar.

To say that it was a strange environment for the gig would be an understatement. I can just imagine some unsuspecting guy walking into the tavern looking for a cold beer and finding an opera concert in full progress. To top it off, MaryAnn Evangelista, nee Bailey, wound up accompanying herself on the piano! The place was jammed.

The people of Ferndale who attended that evening's event will never ever forget it. MaryAnn was such a talent that the crowd in the tavern literally leapt to its feet after nearly every song. She sang for two hours without a break, did several encores, and refused payment or tips for the evening. She paid for everything out of her own pocket for her own homecoming.

I have suggested to the Whatcom Symphony Orchestra that it hire her to come back to sing with the symphony. After all, she deserves a real homecoming. I'm sure that everyone in town would come to support her in performance. I'd be there for sure. It's been a few years and I don't know if MaryAnn is still singing, but if she is, I can guarantee you a night of singing you'll never forget. Maybe she'll come if we tell her that she can ride an escalator.

Two Mysteries Solved

During my first ten years of teaching in Ferndale, I split my day between team teaching band and choir with Al Carr at the high school, and teaching band at the middle school level. Ethel Crook also used me as an assistant conductor for the orchestra. Officially, though, I was director of the Alexander Junior High School and the Custer Middle School bands. My work at the high school was only for two periods a day. Because I was an itinerant teacher, my schedule called for some driving during the school day, and my briefcase was my office. Once, in the faculty room, a teacher asked me what it was that I was selling. She thought I was a salesman working hard to sell someone something at the high school, because she saw me there so frequently and always with a satchel.

One day after school, as Al and I conversed, he recruited me to help him with a problem.

"Someone is stealing my directing batons," he said. Now, those batons aren't expensive, but when you get one that you like, it's frustrating not to find it where it belongs, when you need it to direct. I told him that I would keep a sharp eye out for anyone messing around with his baton while he was not around.

As days went by, there was no activity relative to the baton to report. But a mystery of my own had surfaced, and I told Al that I, too, was trying to find the guy who was poking small holes in my conductor scores. It was very frustrating for me and destructive to the music. I asked him to watch out for that vandal.

With a concert approaching, Al worked diligently to get his band ready for the event. His emotions often would get the best of him as he got into a piece of music, and he would just stop the band to tell them how beautiful it sounded, sometimes with tears in his eyes as he spoke. He truly directed from the heart.

But he also could lose his patience and raise his commanding voice and become as scolding as a football coach with a lethargic team. Well, during band rehearsal one day, he lost it. Instead of tapping the stand with his director's baton, he whacked it. And later in the rehearsal he shouted, "No!" and swung the baton upwards dramatically, clipping the music stand on the way. The baton flipped out of sight. He finished the class without the baton and didn't bother to look for it.

After school, we were again talking near the conductor's podium and I glanced over and saw that someone had punched a small hole in his conductor score.

"Hey Al," I said," It looks like the hole puncher vandal has struck your music."

"He got my baton, too. It's gone."

It was then that I noticed the shape of the hole in the music. It looked as if it was struck with something pointed but on a flat angle to the paper.

"That's strange. Look at the way this hole—" I suddenly realized just who was making the holes in *my* music. It was me. (And Al, in his.) When we would tap the stand, the tip of the baton would bend down as we struck, make a tidy little hole in the music, and then return to its straight position. My mystery was solved!

Al's mystery went on for another week or so, when he again whacked the baton against the stand on the upswing. Again, the baton flipped up and away. Al went on directing without using the baton and was in a bad mood. This time I followed the flight of his baton. When the music stopped, I told Al that I had something very important to tell him. He looked at me and saw that I was smiling and, because he was in a grouchy mood, told me to wait.

I said, "Al, look up!" There in the ceiling of the Ferndale High band room were twelve conductor's baton—I had counted them—stuck in the acoustical tile. It was like someone had told him the funniest story he had ever heard. He laughed until he had to leave the podium and wipe his eyes. The kids laughed too, and it was good for them to see Al laughing and his face so red. The students loved the man.

Like Pogo once said in the comics, "We have met the enemy and they is us!"

Silent Night? Hardly

During the 1960s, I team taught music classes at Ferndale High School for half of the day before working at the junior high in the afternoon. My mentor and colleague, Alvin Carr, had booked his choir into the Seamount Nursing Home but was on the sick list when the gig rolled around. I received a call from Al asking that I take the students up to the home in their concert clothes and just let 'em sing. They know the drill: just stand back and let the kids set up the risers, carry equipment, etc.

"It'll be a piece of cake," he said. All I had to do was lead the choir through twenty minutes of Christmas music and come back to the high school. It sounded easy enough, as the nursing home was only a few blocks away.

"What could possibly go wrong?" I asked myself.

Things were right on schedule, with the kids ready in their fancy duds and the risers set. The choir was left waiting, however, until the attendants could find the small organ we were to use. When it finally arrived, there was a lot of apologizing going on—the organ had not been played in many years. Well, that organ was so quiet we could barely hear it even at full volume, but in the end, it would be used.

First, the television set had to be turned off and patients' chairs turned around to face the choir. None of that went smoothly. Many of the patients didn't understand why their program was turned off. The residents wanted to watch their regular programs and resisted both vocally and physically. But in the end, the attendants won out.

"Hey, it's Christmas!" they said.

The choir was ready to mount the risers and start the show. When the boys stepped up to their accustomed places on the top row, their heads were too high and bumped the ceiling if they didn't bend down. The girls, many in pastel-colored strapless formal gowns, would not step on the risers because of the boys behind them, with their heads bent down over the girls. I understood the situation. Houston, we had a problem. So, I mandated the boys to the front row (amid much complaining) and the girls simply went behind them and filled the risers. That's show business, guys.

Our first song was interrupted when two patients were wheeled in front of the choir and directly behind me as I conducted. They were pretty extreme cases and, although I didn't mind the sight, the students were in a mild state of shock as they performed, looking right at the two invalids in their paralytic conditions.

After a song or two, the sound of a loud scream from down the hall filled the air. As the choir sang "Deck the Halls" they looked down the hall to see what was wrong. A nurse came by and said that all is well but there is a patient who is not happy here and has been screaming on and off during the morning to register her complaint. We tried to ignore the screams as we performed each selection thereafter.

I was introducing the choir's last song, "Silent Night," and thanking the audience for letting us entertain them, when again we heard the woman scream. We began our final song very quietly as the organ was so soft it kept the choir in a quiet tone as well. Nearing the second verse, a woman with a bed sheet wrapped around herself came running down the hall, screaming. I was in the way, so I stepped aside, and she ran by and disappeared out the front door! The choir instantly broke out in tears and barely managed to sing but somehow kept on singing. Male attendants in white uniforms rushed out the front door and, in a matter of seconds, returned with the patient in tow.

To say that this was just about the most pathetic thing we had ever witnessed is an understatement. Even the boys cried.

"Sleep in heavenly peace," the choir sang.

And as the attendants gently yet forcibly hauled the distraught patient back, past the barely singing choir, her screams created further trauma for everyone. The other patients turned on the television and moved their chairs back around.

We beat a hasty retreat for the bus. I had the students remain quiet while I reflected on the situation we had just experienced. It was a good thing to do. The students wanted to talk about the experience, so we simply sat and talked until they were ready to go back to class.

The choir gig turned out to be a little more challenging than the "piece of cake" Al had promised. It was a very long day.

Carpool Daze

In the early 1970s, drivers were shocked to discover that the cost of a gallon of gasoline had doubled in price almost overnight. Somehow, the oil cartel had driven the price up and we simply had to live with the outrageous idea that a single gallon of gas could cost 70 cents rather than the more reasonable price of 35 cents per gallon. What were they thinking?

Anyway, despite all the complaints and cries of civil unrest, the price never went down into that 35-cent neighborhood again. Indeed, teachers had to learn to live with the harsh reality of driving to work and spending a greater percentage of their annual $12,000 paycheck on gasoline and oil products. There was no way around it. The price stayed steady at around 75 cents per gallon for quite a while. It began moving up years later. In fact, the biggest problem folks had in dealing with the problem was that prior to that dramatic increase, the price of gas had remained at 25 cents or less for ten years before gently rising to 35 cents in the early 1970s. Of course, most everybody heard about the folks in Europe and other countries spending as much as a whopping $1.50 or $2.00 per gallon. But just like today, we tend to ignore that bit of statistical information and write it off as something to talk about when you speak to foreigners. Our gas was cheap and that was simply the American Way, end of story.

Well, that was just the beginning of the story for commuters in '74. We started being proactive, which was a new concept in those days. In short, do something before something bad happens, like putting your Rottweiler in the pen before the mailman comes to your door. Or something like that.

The days of the Vista carpool were ones of storied tales of inconvenient truths. The characters in the only Vista carpool were ones who were adversely affected by the cost of fuel and weren't about to let the Arabs take food off their tables for something as common as gasoline. So Mr. Wilson, Mr. Lingbloom, Mr. Keegahn, and myself were a carpool not unlike Dagwood Bumstead's in the Blondie comics.

You should be first advised that I was the last member to join this venture. As such I was subjected to a ritual in which I would swear allegiance to the carpool and put it above all else, including God and family. I think it was tongue-in-cheek allegiance, but I signed on knowing that I'd surely hear from God on this one but my wife would never know, so "Let's boogie on down the road!" I told myself.

The first day of the carpool for me was traumatic. Catching the carpool in the morning was a piece of cake, but I had so many things I had to do after school that when it came time to leave I could barely tear myself away. Somehow I made the effort and got in the car before it began rolling. I must explain. Even if all parties were not in the car, the car rolled slowly away from its parking place at the stroke of 3:00 p.m., and those aboard were going home. Those one minute late would run like the dickens to catch the car, which, by the way, would refuse to stop to let some jive, latecomer dude in. So we became adept at gaining entry to a moving car long before the movie *Little Miss Sunshine* made it a popular pastime.

As the car left the school grounds, we would yell "Incoming!" and throw open the door for the tardy member. Often, when this occurred, the latecomer would simply throw his satchel or handful of papers he had to correct into the car door prior to his own leap into the vehicle. Once in, he was first congratulated for his daring arrival style and later chastised for being late. "Remember your pledge!" Then we would all recite the pledge: "The carpool is first in my life, above God, family, and everything!" I kept waiting for lightning to strike the car after that.

One not-so-fine day the rain was coming down like in the movie *A Perfect Storm*. We were on the freeway just past the Smith Road, going south toward Bellingham, where we lived. Passing a car, we noticed that it was one of our fellow teachers, Mr. Sozanski, in his green Datsun B-210. Someone noticed that his coattail was hanging below the door, which had been slammed on it. The fabric was dragging on the street. It seemed logical to alert him to the problem. I want to tell you that I have never laughed so hard as I did while watching Jay try to figure out what we were pointing at down at the side of his car. The rain was so intense we couldn't roll down the window or stop and tell him. So, literally everything we tried by pointing went unheeded. The next day, Jay told us it was a nice try but his coat was ruined.

Mr. Lingbloom didn't drive his car very much and it was not well maintained. That was in evidence as we progressed toward Bellingham on the freeway one day and were surprised to hear the flapping sound of a flat tire, complete with a wide range of vibratory effects.

"Not to worry, Keith! We're the carpool!"

The tire was fixed in record time, with three guys sharing the duties needed. It was a pit stop. We were soon on our way and patting ourselves on our backs for a job well done when, again, we heard the flap, flap, flap of a flat tire. With no spare and only about a quarter mile shy of the Mount Baker exit, we decided to hoof it to our destination, the K-Mart parking lot, where our cars were parked.

Walking single file along the freeway shoulder, the four of us spotted a car and immediately had the same idea: we'll hitch a short ride. The four of us raised our pant legs and displayed our hairy legs à la Betty Grable. The first car stopped. It was Jay Sozanski in his green Datsun B-210. He gave us a lift to the K-Mart lot, and then it was Mr. Wilson who discovered that he had left his car keys back on his desk at school. Our good friend Jay drove him back to school and then back to his car.

As the year was nearing its end, the teachers had a union meeting at one of the schools. Near the end of the meeting, I had to leave a bit early to meet a music lesson student in Bellingham at my home. I was driving out of the parking lot when I noticed that there were things in my car that didn't belong to me. I stopped. Looking around, I found that although my car was running well, something was wrong. The engine didn't sound quite right. I looked at the papers and found the answer.

I hurried back to the meeting, searched the room, and found the guy I wanted. You see, another teacher and I had identical cars and my key even fit his car's ignition. That car was a green Datsun B-210.

Curse of the Gym Phantom

Voting day induces a wide variety of feelings for most of the population of Whatcom County each year—everything from patriotism to excitement and anticipation to the antithesis of those feelings. In the realm of public schools, prior to Washington State becoming a mail-in ballot state, voting day meant somewhat more. Because the voting places were often held at schools in session, little adjustments needed to be tweaked into the mechanism called "the normal school day."

These usually insignificant accommodations fell directly on the music teachers of the participating schools. Their rooms were the ones most often used for voting. Voting day meant that they would need to find another place to teach for a day. A place that won't disturb, crowd, or in some fashion hinder learning in other classes. Once an alternative room was found, the teacher would go about his/her business until voting day merriment had ceased and then laboriously return all student-moved equipment back to the music room, usually sans student help.

Now, voting days are always on Tuesdays. So are many school concerts. And occasionally the two coincide. For example, the concert on voting day at Custer School in the mid 1980s. To say that I was unhappy to find myself in the boys' locker room, rehearsing the band for the evening concert, would be an understatement. Some of the kids played their trumpets in the shower room! That was fun.

Anyway, as Larry the Cable Guy says, "We got 'er done!"

The "phantom" sometimes struck during concerts. For example, at one band concert, during a quiet section of the music, a music stand was bumped and several percussion traps fell to the shiny gym floor from the back riser with a loud and percussive crash. When the music continued after a brief pause, there came the sound of a tuba mouthpiece hitting the floor. *Bang*! Like a gunshot. (Those mouthpieces are the size of a baseball and made of heavy metal.) The band continued, albeit with trepidation, and was near the end of the quiet part when the drummer's drumsticks began rolling from her snare drum, where they had been stationed while she covered the bass drum part. As she reached to catch the falling sticks, she caught the table-like stand with the orchestra bells, knocking the whole works down with a crashing, tingling, complex mixture of musical sounding noises. The audience's laughter that followed was actually refreshing to hear. I turned and told the audience that we must have a phantom in the gym. Even the students laughed at that line. It seemed that was the very first incident recorded of phantom concert disruptions. It would have gone unnoticed had I not brought the phantom concept into being. I was reminded of the phantom whenever things didn't go quite as planned in a concert after that.

Another example of the phantom's sneaky tricks happened one day at a 1:00 p.m. all-school assembly. The Custer Band was to play a preview concert for the school kids, and an evening concert later that night. In preparation for this, I had the band risers, microphone, and even the band members ready to go and in place by 12:30 p.m. The band warmed up for the concert and still had about ten minutes to spare. I gave the band some down time and admonished the group that they should keep their uniforms clean. Yes, I felt like a mother hen.

With a few minutes left before calling the band to muster, I was approached by a band member as he climbed over the chairs, from the back row toward the director's podium. As for most boys, the "climbing over" method served better than the "go around" method. After I answered his question, he turned around and began going back over the chairs when I told him to go around. As he stopped to follow my request, his foot went down between the chair back and the seat of the old, wooden, folding chair he was stepping over. There came an audible *snap!* followed by the howling of the young man. The phantom of the band concert had struck. This kid was in real pain as his leg had forced itself down, past a metal bar that ensnared him, and the bar was straining against him like the snap ring on my lawnmower. Trying to move the lad was very painful, as was even trying to get the leg out.

The assembly bell rang right on cue and the classes came pouring in. The boy was now suffering from humiliation as well as pain. There was an immediate conference by the attending adults. The janitor—that's it! He'll save the day, we decided. Our custodian, Joe Jensen, could do anything. He alone could solve the Middle East crisis.

But Joe took a look and said, "He needs to be cut out of there."

The student body watched as the Custer fireman, who walked over from the fire station across the street, calmly cut the steel bar with heavy metal shears. Once out, the boy drew the cheers of his schoolmates and tried to walk on the leg. He could, but he had to limp.

I asked him if he felt like playing the concert and he said, “Sure.” So he ambled back to the drum section, figured out a way to get comfortable, and played the gig.

During the evening concert, I was tempted to tell the audience about the unusual earlier experience, wherein the boy was savagely attacked by the folding chair, but I figured I’d better not tempt the Phantom of the Gymnasium.

Students Come First!

The new motto at our elementary school had a nice sound to it: "Our Students Come First!" That motto was ringing in my ears as I heard the message from the office regarding an upcoming election and the music teachers' problems that always accompanied such events.

To begin with, music teachers had to deal with the interruption that came for a day once or twice each year. That usually meant that the students had a recess outside, which was always okay with the kids, just not the music teachers. Teachers had their lessons interrupted on those days, and like many other class interruptions, elementary teachers would simply have to deal with it. But music was different. The music teachers had to surrender their rooms for the local voters to employ their constitutional right to vote. Classroom teachers did not. But the sign said, "Our Students Come First!" Hmm.

Also, in the spring came the annual school musical, involving numerous kids in makeup, singing and dancing for huge audiences. That was the good part. The bad part was that the stage was my classroom and for about a month my band and choir classes had to live with an ever-growing amount of scenery and props to work around. Some of the constructions took up a lot of space on the floor, while others were just there because that's where they were stored for play rehearsals. The scenery and constructions got so intrusive that it began to affect my class. I couldn't see them all. Really, several students were seated behind large stairways, doors, and one huge elevated platform, part of an elaborate altar that had stairs leading to it. By the time of the play I could see only half of my students.

I complained to the principal. I was told that the play was for the students and the sets would not be moved. "So where would you like to take your class?" he offered.

I asked if I could talk to the set builders and maybe we could work something out. That's when he gave me the news: the set was being made by volunteers and Bobbi was in charge. Bobbi is my daughter and had helped all year as a teacher's aide.

The situation was worked out and eventually the play was over and things returned to normal. All the scenery and set construction was gone and I could see my class again. I had missed them so.

Just before the end of the year we spent the last month in a classroom of our own, a portable, one of many in the district that were moved here and there as needed. Evidently it was needed for the coming year. My students loved it. The band had a home! That is, until a message from the principal stated that we would be back on the stage every Tuesday, as the room was needed by the administration for their meetings. Well, we were not happy campers when we heard that. We had band class only three days a week and that meant that we had to haul equipment back and forth. So I complained. Again.

I stood in the office speaking to the school principal as he spelled out the need for the room that we cherished so much. Above me was the sign, "Our Students Come First!" When the principal finished his speech, I simply pointed up.

True to his sign, our band stayed put until the end of the year. The administrators, not we, had to find a place to meet this time.

We had won a temporary battle, but everyone realized the band would be back on stage the next year.

QUAKE
NOTES

One Good April Fools' Day Trick Deserves Another

I enjoy playing jokes, especially on April Fools' Day. I had a class that always enjoyed trying to play an April Fools' Day joke on the teacher. After they tried several times, unsuccessfully, to fool me, we went on through the lesson for the day. Toward the end of the period, a student entered the room and approached me to say that I had a long-distance phone call waiting at the office. Since there were only five minutes left in the period, I figured I could leave the seventh graders for the remaining minutes and take the call. I went down the main hall to the office, but when I got there the receiver was hung up. When I asked why someone hung up my long-distance phone call I learned that, in fact, no one had called me at all. It looked like I had been fooled. I went back up the hall toward my classroom, only to find my class in the hallway laughing and calling, "April fool!" at me. So I hatched a plan of retaliation. The last bell hadn't rung for the class and it gave me an idea.

"Okay," I said, "you got me this time! But I have something to tell you. When I went to the office I heard the principal say that they were going to have a fire drill, and that it would happen any minute. So you need to be prepared to head out when the bell rings." The students quickly pulled the curtains, lined up at the door and waited. I grabbed my grade book for roll call.

A minute later the end-of-class bell rang. (It should be noted that the school bell and the fire bell had one and the same sound. The fire bell was continuous. The schedule bells were not.) The students thought that this was the fire bell and filed out quickly. A light rain was falling. The students waited outside, listening for the next bell to signal an "all clear." I went to the nearby kitchen and poured myself a cup of coffee, returned to my room, sat down at my desk, and put my feet up on it. Eventually, one of the students came back and told me that there were no other classes outside for the drill.

I said calmly, "Tell the rest of the class they are April fools."

So the drenched student went back to tell the others they had been "had." The rest of the students came back in, admitting that I really fooled them that time. I had this particular class for two successive periods, so they were not late getting to another class.

Toward the end of the second period a student came up to me and said, "You really got us good with that April Fools' Day joke, Mr. Storms, but would you do us a big favor? Could you get the eighth graders, too?" I replied that I would if they all promised not to play a joke back on me by letting the eighth graders in on it.

"That's fine," they said. "We really want to get those eighth graders. We would love to have you do it!"

So, I agreed. I told them that they would have to leave the room quickly so that the eighth graders could come in and believe that the tardy bell was, in fact, the fire bell. This they did, and the eighth graders came in and sat down. I explained to them about an imminent fire drill and reminded them of the normal instructions about no running, no talking, waiting patiently outside until the bell rings, and so forth. I grabbed my grade book.

The tardy bell rang and the eighth graders walked outside as directed, stood in the rain, and waited. The seventh graders meanwhile, went through the building to a section where the windows looked out upon the dampening eighth graders, opened the windows, and yelled, "April fools! You dummies!"

The eighth graders returned to the classroom and asked, "Mr. Storms, was that an April Fools' Day joke?"

"Yes, it was. Did they get you?"

"Yeah, they got us good."

I received thank you cards from several seventh graders (okay, two) and I even got a note many years later from some student recalling our prank. It seems they really appreciated a good joke.

Assembly of the Year

During the mid-1980s a Seattle opera program toured Washington schools to promote the appreciation of opera. It's one thing to present a program. It's another to actually get students to attend such a presentation, as the connotation of opera is steeped in misconception. Take for example the well-known case of the "fat lady" and her song. The song she sings has come to represent the end of something. The term "fat lady" recalls the Wagnerian opera singers who sometimes hold spears as they sing and look like Hagar's wife in the comics. All this comes to play in the minds of middle school students. So, knowing this, the powers that be (a.k.a. principals) decided to allow the students a choice of whether to attend the opera singers' concert.

This move proved to be a fine one, indeed, as the students who attended were (1) interested, (2) curious, or (3) eager to get out of class at any cost. Fortunately, the assembly was a success. The students loved the program put on by the four-member squad of opera guys and gals. It wasn't anything like the students expected. In fact, the beauty of the program was . . . well . . . its beauty. Okay, the opera singers were knockouts. The girls went gaga over the male vocalists with their flowing locks and manly statures. Like Greek gods, they were. And the female vocalists entranced the likes of middle school football players to the point where I don't think they cared to know a thing about opera, but the women were knock down, flat out gorgeous, so who cared?

All this fell into a wonderful frame of music provided by the artists. By that, I mean that the kids simply were surprised at what they saw and heard that day. For example, one by one the singers told their stories of getting to the status of opera singers. It was a bit reminiscent of *A Chorus Line*, and it worked. The students were enthralled. The artist/singers were demonstrative, and looks of disbelief swept over faces of everyone in attendance when a soprano showed her skills at high note singing. The applause couldn't have been louder. The kids got it. Opera was not just for old folks. In fact, to drive home that very point, the singers used audience members to create an impromptu opera that had the students first laughing, then stunned, and finally on their feet applauding. What a day!

Well, the students returned to their classrooms and spread the word that the opera singers had just put on the best assembly of the year! And, oh yeah, too bad you missed it.

As assemblies come and go, this one came and went, but it left in its wake a groundswell of interest in opera. Before the end of the week, plans were made to allow students to attend a real, live opera in the Seattle Opera House. With a busload of middle schoolers, a sprinkling of parents, teachers, and yes, even administrators, Vista went to the opera *Aida*. There, we heard the songs that the opera singers sang in our assembly, but within an actual opera. Such songs as "O Patria Mia," "O Terra, Addio," "Ritorna Vincitor," and the one we played in our band class, "Triumphal March," were what the students had awaited.

When I woke up one of the administrators, we prepared to return to Ferndale.

While the students buzzed about going to another opera the next month, word came down that the Seattle SuperSonics basketball team was on a roll. The end of the opera trips came because of a simple choice that was necessary to make. And choose they did. The fat lady sang.

Hold the Horses!

One day in 1968, I rose to my feet with the audience of music educators at the Seattle Opera House, to applaud the performance of junior high school students from Seattle's Sharples Junior High School. I told myself that my very own Vista Middle School students would someday see this act. The act was the African Drum Ensemble and it was fabulous! Talking about the performance could never do it justice, for the combination of talent, creativity, and obvious hard work made this group a unique one, indeed.

I immediately contacted the director of the ensemble and, with the okay from my principal, set up a concert visitation that would involve an overnight stay for the student members and their director.

When the visiting students arrived, our students watched carefully as fifteen black students moved their interesting drum equipment into our school and proceeded to set it up on the stage.

To say that the visitors were nervous would be an understatement. However, after the musicians began their performance things changed a lot. The Vista students not only welcomed them but gave them such enthusiastic applause (as did the faculty) that the Sharples kids simply beamed with pride. All nervousness disappeared. Our students asked for autographs, took pictures, and crowded around them like they were celebrities.

Many staff members commented to me that it was a wonderful performance and thanked me for bringing them to our school. I felt that I had done a real service for our students in bringing the African Drum Ensemble to Vista Middle School.

When school was out that day, the visiting students gathered in small, tight groups in front of the main doors of the school building. As the visitors' names were called, to go with Vista parents for their overnight accommodation, the students didn't budge from their tight circles. Over and over the names were called out, but not one student responded with so much as even a glance in the direction of a waiting car. At first it seemed rather humorous, but that gradually changed to frustration. The ensemble's director first encouraged, then warned, and finally demanded that the students obey. All to no avail. One of their students finally turned and said in a loud voice, "I ain't gonna stay in no white folks' house!" The other students chimed in with agreement.

After nearly an hour of patiently waiting for the students to give in and feeling a bit out of ideas, one parent, Mrs. Dot Nichols, said with a sad sound in her voice, "I guess our horses are going to be without riders tonight, so I'll have to go home and take off their saddles."

Heads snapped around and one girl asked, "Did you say horses? You got horses?"

"Yes," Dot told them, and she said that they were waiting to be ridden before dark. Visitors were in that car quicker than a school of piranhas on a corn dog.

"Hey, you got horses too?" they asked each car.

"No, but we have chickens and cows," said one.

"Wow! Hey, everybody, these folks got cows!"

The remaining students went shopping from car to car, each seeking a farm animal of their choice. In roughly thirty seconds the quandary of dealing with headstrong students was solved.

As the last car left I asked the director if she had ever seen anything like that before.

"No," she said. "These inner city kids are hard to figure. But all we have to remember is that middle school students are thirsting for acceptance, love, security—"

"And horses!" I added.

Some Hat Stories

The Custer Band had lined up for the annual trek down the streets of Bellingham in what was known as the Kiddies' Parade back in the 1970s. All the bands waited their turns, to be signaled by an official's order, "If your band is ready . . . go!" Since each band was just as tired of standing around waiting for those words as the others, all the junior bands of Whatcom County were more than ready to march. But that year I was faced with a unique problem. I know, I know, you're thinking, "Bob, all your problems are unique." Not true, Tonto.

The problem seemed to be with my drum major. He was reluctant to wear a tall drum major's hat in the parade. He didn't know that he would be required to wear it until parade day, because we didn't need it until then. Well, he took one look at that colorful, overblown piece of headgear and simply said, "I'm not wearing that!"

The band in front of ours marched away playing their school song at full volume. That meant we were next, and it would be in just a few minutes when we would hear, "If your band is ready . . . go!" I tried everything to get the guy to suck it up and go down the street wearing the hat. But he carefully removed it from his head and handed the hat, whistle, and mace to me and left.

I turned to the band and met their questioning gaze.

"Anyone want to be the drum major?" I asked? Silence. Then, while standing there staring at each other, we heard it.

"If your band is ready . . . go!"

Again, silence.

Finally, a man came up and tapped me on the shoulder and said quietly, "We're ready for Custer."

Silence.

Finally, a tall girl in the saxophone section said, "I'll give it a try."

She handed me her sax and I gave her the whistle, mace, and the big hat, which she promptly put on. She tried out the whistle and everybody jumped. Even me. She took charge!

She barked some orders that she knew from being in the band, blew the whistle, and proudly led the Custer Band down the street. Afterwards, the students told me that she did a way better job than the student who walked out at the last minute. I was both happy and sad. Happy that the students were gratified with their performance. Sad that a young person had placed so much emphasis on his appearance to the exclusion of his responsibilities to the band. I later told him that he had done a good job for almost the entire marching season and that I was very sorry for not presenting the hat to him earlier. I said that he was not the only one at fault. And . . . that he looked pretty good in the hat.

Vanity played a starring role in the next hat story. And vanity could be considered a central theme in the lives of young people all over the world. After all, looking good is important no matter where you live and what you do. But it's a force to deal with when you are working with young people.

As the Vista Band marched down the street each year, I was well aware that our band was the only band in the Junior Ski-to-Sea Parade that wore hats. On the surface, it doesn't seem like much to ask a batch of middle school students to wear headgear. Trust me, it is.

For example, as we rode the bus to the annual Bellingham competition for all middle school bands in the county, the Junior Ski-to-Sea Parade, the kids were nervous and fussed about with their white clothes, trying haplessly to keep them clean for the parade. The annual question came not unexpectedly.

"Mr. Storms, why do we have to wear hats? The other bands don't wear hats."

I would offer my usual answer, which was a question: "Which band placed first last year?"

"We did!" they shouted.

"Well then, there's your answer."

That little problem was followed by a taunting of the band girls by the girls who carried the flags and banners.

"We don't have to wear hats, do we Mr. Storms?" They knew the answer.

"No, you don't have to wear hats."

And so, the hatless flag bearers taunted the hatted horn blowers unmercifully for the rest of the trip to Bellingham. That is, until the rain began to fall.

The rain came down. It rarely rained on parade day, but this day seemed to be the exception to the rule. Concern for our two months of daily practice to ready ourselves for the day's competition was paramount in the minds of the students. Questions came at me from all sides.

"Will they cancel the parade?"

"Do we walk around puddles or march through them?"

"Can we stay on the bus?"

"When do we eat?"

"Can I sit with Connie?"

The letup of the rainfall around parade time was a signal that we weren't going to get rained out. So the bands all disembarked from their vehicles of mass entertainment known as school buses and began forming their lines (ranks).

I didn't trust the giant, black, mother-of-all, nimbus cloud that rolled in from behind us as we waited to begin our march. And sure enough, just before we were to start, the gigantic nimbus rained on our parade. Correction: Poured on our parade.

The hatted horn blowers found that they were kept dry and relished the protection of an all-plastic hat that covered so much area. The "cowboy hats," as the kids called them, had wide brims on one side, with the other pinned up, Aussie style. By the time we began our march down the street, the hatless flags carriers had begun screaming. They begged for hats. The girls were in double horror as they watched each other's makeup run and their hair, once so carefully prepared, pressed to their faces, dripping and appearing like they had just risen from underwater.

"How come just the band gets hats?" they cried.

I offered them my usual answer: "Which band placed first last year?"

Stravinsky's Rite of the Jedi?

Star Wars came out in the late 1970s. All the kids at school were naturally eager to see the movie, but it hadn't come to our area yet. One lucky student went to Seattle for the preview screening. He bought an LP record of the soundtrack and brought it to school.

So it was, as I opened the door to the classroom the following morning, that some students approached me and told me there was a recording they hoped to listen to, the *Star Wars* soundtrack. I told them that I had planned for them to listen to music that day in class, but that I had planned for them to hear Igor Stravinsky's *The Rite of Spring* instead.

"But we want to hear *Star Wars*!" They protested.

"I'm sorry," I said, "I can't simply change the lesson plan for you guys. We are going to listen to Stravinsky today."

They were not happy to hear it and continued to beg for the *Star Wars* music.

We entered the classroom and I went to get the Stravinsky record. The student with the *Star Wars* album pleaded again to hear his record instead. Finally, I relented.

"Well, I guess we can put off the Igor Stravinsky lesson until tomorrow. I suppose I can do that. Would everyone like to listen to the *Star Wars* soundtrack today instead of the Stravinsky recording?"

Cheers erupted across the classroom. With the class believing that I would now play *Star Wars*, I quietly took the Igor Stravinsky recording of *The Rite of Spring*, put it on the record player turntable, and began to play it. Then I picked up the *Star Wars* album and copied the names of the pieces on the chalkboard, to complete the charade. The students were listening eagerly to Igor Stravinsky while believing that they were actually listening to the *Star Wars* album. They were in rapt attention for twenty minutes.

I could get away with this because none of the students, save one, had seen the movie yet. And I felt that even the student who had seen the movie was unlikely to realize that the recording he was listening to was not from the movie, as it was so new. It also helped that there were the same number of songs on each side of the record. A true coincidence and a helpful one at that.

When the first side finished playing, I had to turn over the record. I asked the students at this point if they wanted to continue listening to the record and they all urged me to keep playing the album.

"Oh, all right," I said. And I played as much as possible until the period was to end.

One student came up to me toward the end of the recording and remarked that they still hadn't heard the theme music which was part of the radio commercial for the movie. I picked up the album and said that it appears that it is the very last piece and we would be hearing it tomorrow. He asked if the music could be played in the last few remaining minutes of the period and I said okay.

I went over to the record player and picked the record up. Feigning surprise, I said, "Well look at that. I haven't been playing *Star Wars* at all! I've been playing Igor Stravinsky's *The Rite of Spring*!" To say that they were shocked would put it mildly.

A student approached me afterward and asked me if that was an April Fools' Day joke, because it was indeed April 1. I told him, "No." I went on to say that the lesson was on the music of Igor Stravinsky, and I played Stravinsky for them. All I did was tell them that it was something different. If I had told them that it was Stravinsky, while they were hoping to hear *Star Wars,* they wouldn't have enjoyed the music at all. As it was, everyone enjoyed it.

The boy nodded, but he looked puzzled. He said, "I don't get it. That music sounded so modern. It sounded like the music we hear in the theaters today. But you say this music was written back in 1912? So why does it sound so modern?"

I replied, "Well, Stravinsky was ahead of his time. Actually, people who listened to his music back then didn't like it very much." This bit of information surprised the boy.

The next day in that class I played the real *Star Wars* album. At the end of the period a student came up and said, "I don't understand. Why do the two records sound alike? I couldn't tell the difference between them."

I had never realized before how similar they were.

"I guess that John Williams, the composer of the *Star Wars* soundtrack, probably studied Igor Stravinsky a great deal earlier in his music career."

Listen to *The Rite of Spring* and to the *Star Wars* soundtrack for yourself, and see if you don't agree.

T.U

Snowy Day "Special"

You know it will be a great day in school when you're looking at a foot of new snow on the bus loop. The students will be on buses a half hour late and wound up tighter than a high C string on the piano. It's all part of teaching school, and teachers deal with it in many ways. Some of those ways actually work.

One snowy day in early February, our students came an hour late. Within just a few minutes they were all nestled in their cozy, warm classrooms and out of the freezing weather. They had gone through the usual rituals—flag salute, lunch count, and attendance—and were just getting down to business when a rather dramatic principal's voice came on the intercom.

"Attention, everyone! Just now I would like your classes to come to the front windows and see something that is very unusual and educational as well. It's something special!"

Within seconds the students were out of their seats and lining the windows that looked out onto the bus loop. There in the loop was a family on a large toboggan pulled by a perky brown horse. Father with the reins, mother with her hands on the two children—it was a picture postcard photo op. The principal's message was spot on; the kids were wowed and the cheering began. The family waved and stayed in place as the principal shot pictures of the event. It was like a page out of a storybook from the 1800s or a Hallmark moment.

Meanwhile, the class in a portable on the far side of the building heard the message and began to get ready to see the "special, unusual something" that the principal invited them to come and see. So the next few minutes were filled with first graders donning their winter duds, more than a few minutes were filled with them trudging through the snow, and finally, the last few minutes were spent walking the length of the school hallway. Single file. Eventually, the class was stationed appropriately at the front windows where the teacher instructed the class to look out and see just what the "special, unusual something" was.

I wanted to tell the teacher that the "special" had left the scene, but she was so intent that I let her do her thing with the class. She was in charge.

It got rather quiet along the windows as the students watched and searched the area. At last, seemingly out of frustration, a boy asked, "Teacher, why are those dogs doing that?"

After a glance out the window in the direction he was pointing, the teacher drew back and said nothing. She looked around, saw me, and said in a kindly, musical voice, "Mr. Storms would you do me a favor and walk my class back to my room in the portable at the end of the building?"

I agreed, lined up the kids, and began my journey down the hall leading the now quizzical first graders back to class. We were halfway down the hall when we began hearing the teacher's voice as she shouted and ranted at the principal, her musical voice absent. That's when I knew it was time for a song.

"Oh, the farmer in the dell, the farmer in the dell, hi-ho the merry-o, the farmer in the dell!"

It's Alarming

The day was overcast and it looked like rain at Vista Middle School. That's not big news around these parts, but the weather is always a consideration when staging a fire drill at school. And as a light rain began to fall, the bell rang for a fire drill.

"Outside, quickly!" I said. It seemed our students were getting somewhat lethargic and apathetic when it came to fire drills. There was no sense of urgency to exit the classrooms and no lively movement toward the play field.

"Everyone move up on the play field! Let's go!"

The students dragged their feet and nothing seemed to make them move. Of course, eventually, the kids lined up and the teachers took attendance and sent runners to the front of the building to report their class's attendance. And the rain came down. The bell was a long time in ringing that day and students got quite a soaking. We all complained and then went on to our classes.

On another day, our nerves were jangled again by the sound of the fire alarm. "Outside, quickly!" I said. Just as before, the students were in no great hurry to get to their appointed places outside and walked from the school to the playground at a snail's pace, talking and laughing. As the crowd of four classes poured out of the building, a fire truck came around the corner with its siren a-wailing. I'm here to tell you that you have never seen a hundred kids run for their lives as fast as those students did that day. You see, there was a real fire and it seemed to me that the old story of crying wolf had too often come to real life. There was a lesson learned that day.

The next story is one that could have been a tale of a real disaster. It was somewhat associated with school, but only in passing.

One rather dry, windswept day later in the winter, as I was having lunch with Vista principal Bruce Berry, the door opened and Betty Peterson, the school secretary, entered saying that Mrs. Berry had a grass fire in her back yard. It seemed that some coals from the burn barrel had sent sparks to the surrounding dry grass. We both responded like true firemen and were out the door before you could say "Nicci nicci tumbo nosorumbo oomamoochi yamma yamma goochy." The lunch period was but a half hour and I said that I needed to get back as soon as the firemen came. Mr. Berry drove like a house afire to his lawn afire.

When we arrived, the fire had nearly circled the house. Bruce ran inside to get a hose. He had kept it inside so it wouldn't freeze. I grabbed my topcoat—yes, teachers wore those to school in those days—and began fanning the flames away with it. Surprise! it blew out the fire in front of me like candles on a birthday cake. I continued around the house blowing out six foot squares of fire. As my coat was close to getting ruined, I traded the coat for the large rubber doormat off the porch and picked up where I left off with the fire. Bruce, meantime had worked his way around the back side and was coming toward me as the fire truck arrived.

We were both back at Vista in no time, and as I opened the band room door, a student asked me why I smelled like smoke. "I'm a heavy smoker," I said jokingly.

"C'mon, you don't smoke," he said.

"Would you believe that I just put out a big fire, on my lunch hour?"

"That's impossible. There's no fire around here."

"Okay, how about this? I got these clothes at a fire sale?"

"A fire sale? Hmm. I don't know what that is, but I guess that would explain it."

Kids.

AL'S
HORN
REPAIR
I BRAKE FOR
BROKEN BRASS

Let Joe Do It

Everybody in Custer knew Joe Jenson. He was the school custodian for many years. As a vital part of the inner-workings of the school, Joe was not only adept at doing his job but he was also a source of knowledge, friendship, comfort, skills, and entertainment.

To begin with, Joe was a difficult person to understand. That was because, as I recall someone telling me, he was shell-shocked in the war. His speech was such that many people could literally not understand him. And as Joe spoke he had to cover his mouth because he would spit saliva as he talked. That was perfectly acceptable, though, as Joe was worth listening to. His experiences and solutions were edifying to all who listened.

Joe's approach to his job, it seemed to me, was a bit of a cross between being Radar on *M*A*S*H* and a fairy godmother to the school. You say you need something? Check your closet; Joe put one there before you asked. If there was a problem to be solved, Joe was the one to solve it. With his expertise in many fields, Joe was found to be a capable repairman, plumber, and a host of other designations. On his own, Joe planted and cared for the hundreds of flowers that graced the entire front of the building. If you drove by his home, just a block away, you would see his entire home surrounded with a dazzling display of flowers, well cared for and all in bloom. He bought the flowers for the school each year to make his school as nice as his home, or vice versa.

The entertaining part of Joe's personality was simply that he loved jokes and especially practical jokes. His favorite joke, as I remember, was when he would stand near the trays of freshly made clay that the younger grades used, saying nothing as a teacher would get coffee next to the trays. Invariably, the teacher would inquire about the wet-looking clay. Joe would say, "It does look wet, doesn't it?" And when you stuck your finger in it to see if it really was wet, he would quickly grab your wrist and plunge your hand down into the clay. Then he would laugh like a hyena with a hernia. And then he would smooth the clay down for the next victim. Joe got his comeuppance when a feisty female teacher simply turned around and wiped the clay all over his overalls. Front and back!

He also filed off the knob of one of his window sticks, greased it and placed it in a new teacher's closet. He did this so that the new teachers would need to have him come and show them how to properly open a window because the window stick thingy didn't work. He would then say, "The teachers nowadays are just not trained like the ones when we were kids. Why don't they even teach 'em to open a window?" He would simply tell them to leave the job to him. Eventually, he would secretly trade the window stick with a different one and move on to the next victim. Joe pulled it on me when I was a new teacher, and years later he confided in me that he had been pulling that prank on new teachers for a long time but had never told anyone except the principal. I promised not to tell anyone.

The bees' nest in the old gym was Joe's pride and joy. It was so huge. He told me that for a few years, professional beekeepers came and dealt with the nest and the honey. It was costly. One time, Joe and a helper had decided to do the job themselves and keep the honey. With bee suits and equipment for working with bees, the men climbed the ladders into the bees' nest. Not surprisingly, the bees gave them the full treatment. The men carried on pretty well until a single bee got into the helmet of the helper, so he had to take off the helmet. He nearly fell as he panicked, but was able to dismount the ladder and run for the main building just twenty feet away.

Once inside, he thought he was safe but found that the bees had followed him into the building. He ran wildly through the halls, with the bees chasing him, while Joe laughed hysterically. When the helper returned up the hall, with the bees still after him, Joe dove into the boys' lavatory. The helper came in, too, and they were safe. But trapped. The bees stayed outside for a long while before finally seeing the sun go down. They gave up and tried to get back to the nest. But now, the bees were trapped in the school. The two men left in their bee suits and called it a day. Joe swept up the bees the next day.

Joe's good friend and principal of Custer School was Roland Peterson. Rollie was dependent on Joe for many things and appreciated his work and his dedication to the school and the district. When a new superintendent came and changed things around, Rollie went to bat for Joe and tried to keep things as they were, but it was not to be, and soon Joe was joined by a helper who was to take over some of Joe's responsibilities.

After being trained by Joe, the worker had half of the building to maintain and Joe had the other half. This arrangement was sensible to the casual observer or on paper, but it took Joe's heart out of the job. The other guy didn't work to the standard that Joe required and, to make matters worse, Joe's flowers were all pulled out and shrubs were planted in their place. The new superintendent said that the maintenance crew was to do that work, not the custodian. That was not a happy day, I can tell you, the day the flowers came out.

When Joe passed away, a little bit of Custer's history went with him as he was simply an unusual man. One that put fun and pride into his work. We need people like Joe in every profession, I think. Even teaching, for as we know, Joe taught the teachers how to open their classroom windows. I miss him.

Lights Out! Action!

One day in the early 1980s, just after school had started at 8:00 a.m., the lights went out at Vista Middle School. In many places, that would not be cause for alarm, but at this school, where windows were few and emergency lighting hadn't arrived yet, it was a genuine fiasco.

The trouble started as soon as the lights went out in my band room. Students screamed at the tops of their lungs, and some left their chairs and began groping around in the darkness. I'm here to tell you that room went absolutely pitch black. In fact, I got completely disoriented trying to find the door to the hallway. I wound up in the instrument storage room. When I finally got out of there, I realized where the door must be and subsequently found it. Dim light streaming in from a dark hallway was enough to get my class out and down to the cafeteria, where there were windows and more light. The day was overcast, and even with the drapes pulled back, half of the cafeteria was still in the dark.

As we waited for the lights to come on, the class heard students in other classes screaming and running around in the darkness. Because I couldn't see all of my students all of the time, some slipped off into the darkness to join the madding crowd. I was helpless to keep control of the class. Kids came and went amidst the screaming that seemed to ebb and flow, like a tide going in and out. I knew that if I were to tell my class to stay there while I tried to round up my wayward students, I would return to an empty space where I left them. I stayed put.

More classes arrived and soon groups of students began to sing. The singing helped, I think, because other students began to think that there was some organization, and perhaps even light, where there was singing. So out of the darkness they came until most of the school was assembled there. The administration issued instructions and sent runners with flashlights to tell the teachers the next move. The hard part was to get the message to the students who were busy taking advantage of their newfound freedom amidst the chaos.

It seems a car had collided with a power pole on Vista Drive, and we learned that the power would be out for about an hour. It felt like an hour had passed, when indeed, it was only fifteen minutes or so.

Meanwhile, back at the ranch, the little darlings were still out of control and the word got around that it would be an hour before the lights came on. Teachers resigned themselves to do their best to keep their classes together by taking attendance by flashlight. Well, just as soon as attendance was taken, off students went into the screaming darkness. It was a long morning.

After a while, the screaming subsided a tad and the students in my visible class began to tell ghost stories. There wasn't a lot of objection to this because all the students needed to do, if they were bored with the ghost story idea, was to steal off into the darkness. Keeping my class together was a bit like trying to keep hop-toads in an open box.

When the lights came on around 11:00 a.m., we were all exhausted. That it was all over was the good news. The bad news was that we hadn't even finished half a day's work. But the screaming and running around was history.

The potential for a bad accident was definitely there during that time, but we were lucky no one was injured and nothing was broken during the emergency. Our staff, upon a time of reflective evaluation following the event, did some serious thinking about helpful changes that were needed in an emergency such as this. Among the first of those changes was the request for emergency lighting. Granted. I suggested a bottle of aspirin, earplugs, glow-in-the-dark student bracelets, and a flashlight for each teacher. We got the flashlights.

One Ferry Boat, 170 Kids, 125 Tickets

In late February of 1985, the band and choir of Vista Middle School took a trip out to Friday Harbor, San Juan Island, to play for a school concert. It was a big affair, with 170 of our students riding four buses and connecting on a ferry, with the ferry commute about one-and-a-half hours each way. When the concert was over, I turned the students loose in the downtown port of Friday Harbor to let them find some lunch, but with the instructions to meet back at the ferry dock by about 4:00 p.m., to catch the ferry for home.

The ferry we had planned to board for home, however, had engine troubles and was taken out of service. Instead, a substitute ferry about half the size of the original was sent to take over. I was told that this smaller ferry would not be taking on any buses, which was a problem because we had brought the students in four busloads. Then I was told that the ferry would take foot passengers, but only two hundred of them, plus a few cars.

When I learned this news, I became quite upset because I wasn't sure how I would be able to get all the students back home. So I went to the purser's office at the terminal, and he informed me that I would possibly have to find housing for the students overnight. I protested that these were middle school kids and no one was prepared to spend the night. We had no means to put them up anywhere. He replied with, "That's not my problem."

I turned to the school's vice principal, who was traveling with us, and explained the situation. He suggested that we call the school back on the mainland and ask them to arrange for buses to come to meet us when we got off at the other end. This was a good idea, so I returned to the purser and told him that I needed one hundred and seventy tickets, for the band and choir students, and wished to purchase them in advance so that everyone could be ready to walk on the boat.

He replied, "I can only give you about one hundred. The rest have to go for other people."

I told him that there was no way that I could leave seventy students behind. His response was simply, "That's not my problem."

Feeling frustrated, I asked to borrow his phone. While standing in his office, which was adjacent to a small waiting room that could hold only about twenty people, I could see that the sun was starting to go down. Being February, it was already cold and was now getting colder with the disappearance of the sun. In a matter of half an hour, my students were going to be in the cold, and the dark.

I called the principal of our school, who said that he could get some buses down to the dock to meet us on the other side, but was understandably concerned about having any students left behind. Speaking to him on the phone, I hatched an idea.

To the confusion of the principal, I said a little loudly to him on the phone, "I don't know. I'll get his name, title, and badge number."

Then I turned to the purser and asked him for the information. He gave it to me, and I repeated it into the telephone to the principal, whose response was, "What in the world are you talking about?"

The purser was curious now, as well. He asked me why I wanted to know his name, title and badge number. I explained to him that the school principal wanted to know the name of the person who was not letting the students board the ferry, so that when the lawsuit came they would know who was responsible for making the decision. Of course the principal heard this on the phone and began laughing. I covered the phone and then continued to convey my bleak outlook for the close of the day with no help from the ferry personnel.

"I don't know what you're up to, Storms, but go with it!" said the principal, who seemed to be quite entertained by the aspect of some quirky answer to our problem.

As I continued to talk with the principal, the purser interrupted me and said, "Look. I can give you 125 tickets, but that's all. That's really the best I can do." I told him fine, I'd take the lot. So he gave me one hundred and twenty-five tickets. The principal heard the deal go down and was laughing as we closed the conversation.

Now, the vice principal, who was a chaperone, did not know what I was planning, but I had told him to get the buses down to the docks and I'd get the students on board.

I went back to join them and stood up on the first step of one of the buses and had the students gather around. I looked out on the crowd of students and made my speech.

I told the kids, "The good news is that we do have tickets to ride the ferry," and everyone cheered. I continued, "But the bad news is that there aren't enough. There're only 125 instead of 170." There was a shocked silence.

While they were trying to figure out what this might mean, I shouted, "Here's your tickets!" and threw all of them as hard as I could above their heads so that they rained down like confetti. Everyone scattered and tried to pick up a ticket. (I figured that would be the easiest and most fair way to distribute them.)

After a minute, I asked them, "Who has a ticket? Hold it up." And the students who had a ticket held it up. "Here's what we're going to do," I said. "Someone's going to announce very soon that the walk-ons will board first. The gate will go up and the walk-ons with tickets will go on before the cars. We are leaving our music instruments on the buses, and everyone is going to simply walk on the ferry instead of riding on the bus. Except for one important thing: you are not going to walk. When that bar goes up and it is announced that walk-ons can board, all of you are going to run. You are not going to hand your ticket to the man who collects them, you are going to throw it up in the air at him and let him pick it up off the ground. Don't stop, but go on board and on upstairs. He can't stop all of you, and he won't know which of you gave him a ticket, so just keep going."

The students lined up at the gate, and when the bar lifted for the walk-ons to board, there were 170 kids all rushing down the lane toward the boat. There was one man standing in the middle of the path to collect tickets, completely dumbfounded, as the swarm of students came running toward him. The students did as they were told and threw the tickets up in the air as they went by him. They didn't stop, but went on board and upstairs into the seating area and sat down.

The chaperones and I also went on, walking casually with the rest of the other passengers. We handed the fellow our tickets and boarded, but we were not hassled by him because he did not know I was the band director and that the others were the band chaperones.

We got back to the mainland where we were met by other school buses, which took us back home.

I figured that if the purser ever wanted to figure out which students did not have a ticket, that was not my problem.

Music for Every Child

On the first day of school one year, at Mountain View Elementary, I watched the students exiting the bus in their new school clothes and smiled as each student returned to school. One small child was wearing a helmet and needed some help to get down the stairs on the bus, and so the driver assisted him. It was then that I saw why the student needed assistance. He had no arms.

That child, after a few years, wound up in my fourth-grade singing class, and I found that he was not only a very nice boy but a good singer as well. I encouraged him to follow his musical talent. Not surprisingly, he joined the middle school choir and was stationed in the front row center for each concert that the choir performed. I told Mr. Potts, the director of the Vista choir, that the lad was kind of a favorite of mine because he did so well with his apparent handicap and was quite a nice fellow. Mr. Potts agreed and said that he was a real contributor to the choir and he was glad that he was doing so well.

The next year brought a rather unusual problem to my door. Someone was kicking it. When I answered the "knock" I found our armless vocalist standing there. He asked to come in and subsequently asked if he could join the band. Now, I was delighted, but I hesitated and asked him about his choir experience and his fine singing voice. He said simply that he always wanted to try an instrument but was never given the opportunity like other kids because of his handicap. "Choir was good, though", he said. I told him that I would try to figure out something for him so that he could participate. It has been my philosophy to give every child a chance to make music and exclude none. The Music Educators' National Conference (MENC) has a slogan, "Music for Every Child and Every Child for Music," and I bought into it early in my career.

I worked on a solution. "Okay, the guy needs to play an instrument. Wait a minute, every band instrument I can think of needs hands to hold it and fingers to play it," I reasoned. After a long time, I finally gave up and wandered to the main office in search of some help in the matter. I told the principal, vice principal, and counselor about the issue, but none could come up with any help. Back at my desk, I stared out into the band room searching for an answer. My eyes fell on the set of drums in the back of the room. "Nah, he'd need sticks to play the drums. Hmm . . . but if he were to play only the bass drum he could use his foot to play the pedal. Eureka! That's it!" I told myself. "If this works, I'll have done a real service for the young boy."

It worked.

My armless bass drummer performed admirably all year until marching season, when he again graced my door, which happened to be open this time. He asked what he could play in the marching band as he was aware that he would be unable to perform unless he was sitting down. Again, I asked him to let me work on it.

"I don't want to just march in the parade. I want to do something," he said as he was leaving the room.

Again I asked for some help, and this time someone said, "See if he could ride in a golf cart and wave a flag." (The lad had a finger on one shoulder. He could do a lot with it, including feeding himself.)

When posed with the solution we came up with, he said, "That sounds like fun!" It was settled.

I worked out a loan of a utility vehicle, slightly larger than a golf cart, from the City of Bellingham, which delivered, drove, and returned the vehicle. A nifty sign was placed on the front announcing the Vista Middle School Band and Drill Team. The kid was thrilled and went through the parade like a real trooper, waving a small American flag for all his worth. I don't remember if the band won a trophy or not, but I remember the joy that was shown on the young man's face as we performed.

When I look back on the experience, I often think how easy it would have been for me to just say, "You know, I'm really sorry, but there's just nothing here that you can play." But then, I would have missed one of the true joys of teaching: finding ways to help every child succeed and then watching them do just that.

And sometimes an experience comes late in a teaching career and provides education for the teacher more than the student. The following experience was one of those for me.

While walking toward the school office to speak to the principal one day, I was stopped by a cute, little girl with shoulder-length, brown hair. She wore a blue dress and looked a bit like a 1950 catalog ad for the latest school clothes.

"Hello, Mister Music Man," she said.

"Well, Hello to you!"

"When I get in the sixth grade, I'll play the French horn!" she said, as though it were a fact.

Her enthusiasm and determination was quite unusual for a girl I estimated to be a second grader. It is also notable that her choice was the French horn, as it is rarely the first choice of beginners in band class. It is also one of the most difficult instruments to play.

I would only see the young lady a few times a year and it was usually just a wave from down the hall. She was still making me aware that she hadn't forgotten her intention to play in the band.

A few years later, I was ready to seeing her come into my room to join the beginning band as a sixth grader. Beside my desk I had a nearly new French horn for her to play. The anticipation was a wonderful thing, as I knew how much this little girl wanted to play the instrument of her choice. I visualized her opening the case and seeing this beautiful instrument. It would be like Christmas morning!

Right on time, the class entered. My little French Horn player was first in the door. Straight to the desk she came, eyes wide and wearing a big smile. Just as I had envisioned.

"Did you get me a French horn?" she asked.

"I sure did. Come over here to see it."

As she walked around my desk to the place where the instrument was strategically placed, she put her left hand on the desk to leaned down to see the case with the instrument inside. Her hand had no fingers, only a thumb. My heart fell into my shoes as I realized that this little girl could never play the French Horn. It is only playable from left to right, using only the fingers of the left hand. Christmas morning vanished in the blink of an eye. Telling her of this fingering problem would be one of the most difficult things I would ever do in my years of working with school children.

As the girl reached for the instrument, I said, "Wait. I really need to talk to your mother before I check out the instrument to you."

"Can I look at it?"

"Can you wait until tomorrow?"

"Okay," she said, in a falling voice that sounded like she was resigned to have to stay in from recess or something. It was not a good solution but it bought me some precious time.

"Her mother had better be home," I muttered later that day, as I dialed. And fortunately, she was.

I told the girl's mother that it will be impossible for her daughter to play the horn because of her lack of fingers on her left hand.

The lady replied, "Let her try."

"I don't like to see a child cry in my band class simply out of frustration in playing the instrument," I said. "Can we move her to a trumpet? The valves are played with the right hand so she will only have to deal with the problem of holding the instrument with the left hand."

"Let her try," she said calmly, with a determination in her voice that matched her daughter's.

I was about to give up.

"Let her try," she said again.

"But it's impossible!" I said with a last gasp at convincing her.

"Let her try," she said with a tone of submission. She was evidently through trying to convince me.

"Okay, I'll let her try."

The next day when the class came in I decided to tackle the problem head on. The whole class needed to know that the young lady was facing a serious challenge that would be harder for her to deal with than for anyone else in the band class. I opened the case and showed the beautiful French Horn to the class and they all clapped! They were well aware of her desire to play the horn and were happy for her. I was so happy at that show of support by the class that my heart leapt with joy. Christmas morning was back!

In the months that followed, the girl's progress was halting at first, and then rapid for the rest of the year. She found that she could use her thumb to press the first valve, second valve, or both. On the horn, the first two valves are needed to play the majority of notes. The occasional use of the third valve was a separate problem that she somehow figured out.

I retired the following year and later heard that the little girl went on to play French horn in the solo and ensemble contest.

"Let her try" was a simple lesson that this teacher had to learn. And like my experience with the lad who had no arms, my philosophy of "music for every child and every child for music" was tested. "Let her try" was a lesson that spoke of what people with handicaps have to deal with on a daily basis. For those of us who don't have to face these problems, it might seem harsh in its style. But to a young person with a handicap it means just another hard challenge to win.

Music, the Universal Language

During my band class one day, the door opened and my friend Ken Colvin walked in carrying a package. I was surprised to see Ken, as he had been away in the service and had never been to my band room before. After greeting him I turned to the class and introduced my friend. I was happy to see Ken, a fine saxophonist, and was wondering just what brought him to my door.

"I just got out of the service and have been stationed in Japan for the past year," he said. "While I was there I bought some Japanese band music. I was just wondering if your students would like to play the music. I would like to hear it, actually."

At that point I turned to the students and asked them if they would like to play this foreign music. The class responded with a resounding, "Yes!" Ken gave me the package of music, asked me when I thought the band would be up to playing it, and waved to the students as he left the classroom. Nice guy.

When I passed the music out to the students, I noticed the looks on their faces. I marked it up to curiosity. But it turned out the title of the piece was written in Japanese and the band students were only wondering just what the music was about. I told them that a title doesn't always reveal the nature of a piece of music. To be honest, I wanted to know what the title meant as well.

Time passed, and the students had played the two songs long enough to decide whether to use them in a concert. They voted to do only one of the songs, and subsequently I called my friend Ken to inform him of the concert date when he could hear his music performed.

I tried to find out what the title meant, but I didn't know anyone who could interpret the Japanese characters. So on the concert night I had to admit to the audience that I didn't know what the song was about. I told them that it really didn't matter. "Just enjoy the music," I said. I also told them about Ken and his dropping by to lend us the music.

As the final notes sounded throughout the cafetorium, it occurred to me that something as common as a song title can leave people grasping for something to hang on to as they listen to a song being performed. That was not to be, but I told the audience that something else had been learned—simply that our students can enjoy the music when it is played, and our students can follow the instructions in the music the same as our own, because the instructions for all music around the world are written in Italian. This standard was established to facilitate the performance of music around the world without having to necessarily learn a new language.

So, let's see. We wound up having American students playing Japanese music and using instructions written in Italian for our St. Patrick's Day concert. It turns out that the music was not a lot different than our own music and didn't have strange sounds or unusual effects. When Ken finally came to pick up the music, we still hadn't found the title's translation.

It seemed to me that the experience taught us all a lesson about music. I guess that the old saying is true, "Music is the universal language."

Dressing in the Dark Leads to Daylight Fun

Early in my teaching career I was beset with a continuing problem. Because our new tiny babies would always be lodged in our bedroom, for convenience, I had to dress for school in the dark each winter morning, so as not to wake a sleeping babe. My clothes were always laid out the night before, with the decisions about what to wear to school done in a lighted room. This procedure continued over the span of six years and five children. I was used to it.

One Monday, while on my way down the hall to retrieve my mail at the Custer School office, I passed a band student who, upon greeting me proceeded to ask why I was wearing two different shoes. Looking down at my shoes I realized that I was, indeed, wearing one black shoe and one brown shoe. While the student giggled, I made a feeble attempt to explain my dressing-in-the-dark routine. The student went away smiling, and I was doomed to spend the day wearing the mismatched shoes and incurring a pattern of questioning, teasing, explaining, and embarrassment. When I got home and told my wife the story of my day, she added an out-loud laughter component to the series.

I made my perfectly matched shoes appearance the next day at Custer and once again hoofed it down the main hall to get my mail. I passed a sign that said, "Don't be the only one! We're having lots of fun! Come on everyone—wear mismatched shoes on Crazy Shoes Day this Thursday!" It seemed awfully coincidental that my mismatched shoes day was to be followed by a Crazy Shoes Day shortly after, when I had not heard of such a day before. Upon asking the kids I found that my shoes, indeed, had spawned the idea for the new activity. Obviously, with students watching you as closely as that, you'd better be careful.

Well, Crazy Shoes Day wasn't the biggest activity of the year, but it was fun enough to make it to a second-year observance and, once again, I was teased about being the goof that caused the day to happen. I guess in a way I was fortunate that it turned out to be something as harmless as mismatched shoes and not bumping my head into a door or smashing my fingers in a doorjamb. The little darlings might have come up with, "Don't be the only one! We're having lots of fun! Come on everyone . . . !"

Mystifying April Fools' Day Joke

Paging through a music magazine one day in the early 1990s, I spotted a new product that looked interesting. It was a wireless microphone box. For only ten dollars you could buy this gadget and connect your microphone to your speaker system through this little box. It was the size of a pack of cigarettes. Well, since I used a mic and sound system in class to speak to my large band classes, which often ran from eighty to a hundred students each, it looked like something useful and it was only ten bucks, so I ordered it.

The wireless box ran through my stereo system in the band room via the FM radio band. When I hooked it up I had my doubts, but it worked like a charm the very first time I tried it. I wasn't quite sure how I was going to use it, but it seemed to be something I could use down the line in my class. And it was only ten bucks.

April Fools' Day was coming up and I finally had an idea about how to use my new toy. First I checked how far the signal would carry. I asked the janitor to stand outside my door as I walked down the hall talking on the microphone. He was to tell me when my voice stopped projecting from the speakers in the band room. I was impressed but still not sure how I could use the new wireless connection in class.

Standing in my office I could look out into the band room and see everything in the room, but it was difficult for anyone in the room to see into my office. I asked the custodian if he could see me in there. After a long look, he said, "No." What that meant to me was that I could hide in there and instruct my band without being physically present in the classroom. It sounded like a good plan and I was eager to try it out.

When April Fools' Day arrived, I was ready to go. I had the volume set just right, with the custodian's help. All I needed was a plan. Well, that plan took shape as the students came in the door and sat down to warm up their instruments for the beginning of class. When the bell rang for the start of class the students looked around to see if I was coming in the door, but seeing no one, they continued to warm up their instruments and wait.

From my hiding place in my office I calmly instructed the students to stop playing and turn to the warm-up, "Chorale Number 19" in the Raymond Fussell band book. Although they were slow in responding, they did, and I began to count off to start the music. The students continued looking around trying to find who was speaking because it sure sounded like the teacher's voice. Then, most of the students began to play "Chorale Number 19." I said, "Stop! Stop!" and the band stopped playing. I said, "It looks like we need a director, so Janie would you conduct please?" Since the students loved to direct the band there was little hesitation on Janie's part and soon the band was playing "Chorale Number 19."

But as the band played, some of the students put down their instruments, got out of their chairs, and began looking around the room. They looked through the instrument storage room, the three sousaphone cabinets (each of which could hold a person), and even peeked into my office with their noses up to the glass trying to find me. I told them all, by name, to get back in their seats and play the chorale. They quickly responded by racing to their chairs, knowing that I could somehow see them! Next, I asked Janie to direct one of the band's favorite songs, and while they were playing it I walked into the classroom.

I stood and watched them as they performed. When they finished playing, I told Janie that she had done a good job of directing, and I told the students that they were doing a great job of being good citizens by staying in their chairs when the teacher was out of the room. The students who had been out of their chairs looked quizzically at each other. I looked at them.

Without another word, I just took over my job of teaching the band. During class, no one said anything until later, when one student asked, "Where were you, Mr. Storms?"

I said, "April fool!" That answer didn't satisfy them of course, so I promised I would tell them the next day after I played the same joke on the next class. If they told the next class that it was in for an April Fools' Day joke, I wouldn't tell them how I did it.

The following day I did a demonstration using my new wireless microphone gadget. Although it had worked fine the day before, we encountered a built-in problem that I had not anticipated. From the speakers in the room came the sound of a church service somewhere in progress, complete with music sung by a gospel singer. Okay, that drew a few laughs by everyone, including me. It seemed the wireless would occasionally broadcast a local radio station rather than my voice. Hmm, well, if that had happened the day before it would've ruined my April Fools' Day joke, but my luck held and I had indeed pulled it off. Twice, actually.

Then I put the wireless microphone gadget away for good. And although I never used it again, I still savor the day that I had so much fun mystifying the band students and watching them follow my instructions, despite my absence in the classroom. And it was only ten bucks.

No Noise Is Sweeter Than a Low B-Flat

As the 1970 school year began, visitors came to see a new concept in educational design and the architecture of this new-fangled idea called the "open-concept" middle school. The visitors from Japan and Canada represented a fraction of the worldwide interest generated by this new concept. The school was not ready to open on schedule, but open we did, and our classes were often interrupted by the sounds of hammers, electrical tools, saws, and everyone's favorite, the jackhammer. Add to that fire drills and class bells that rang at the wrong times and you get the picture.

Our visitors got a look at a school in the making and it wasn't pretty, let me tell you. For instance, my band class was held in a science room that was empty at that hour, because the band room was nowhere near completion. It was a distinct challenge to try to teach/entertain a crowd of eighty-plus band students who were not allowed to play their instruments for a couple of weeks.

One day, when at last I was teaching in my band room, a group of visitors from a school district in Japan came through—in one door, across the room, and out the other door—and were interested in watching me teach the band class. The new school had brought with it brand new instruments, and it was my job to teach the students how to play such things as a tuba, sousaphone, baritone, oboe, bassoon and a baritone saxophone.

As the visitors watched, my baritone sax student was trying very hard to make a low B-flat come out of her shiny, new, oversized saxophone. Time after time she tried to no avail.

"Gloria, follow my instructions." I said. I repeated them and again there was nary a peep out of that big saxophone. The superintendent was guiding this group of visitors, nudging them toward the exit door, but the drama of the moment kept our visitors riveted in place.

At last, I tried another approach and said, "Look, open your throat like you are swallowing an egg and blow!" The sound of a glorious, low b-flat emanated from that shiny contraption and took everyone by surprise with its sonority. The burst of applause from our visitors signaled the students to cheer and applaud as well. Gloria was off the hook. She had been near tears trying to get the darned thing to operate, and when she finally did, her face was lit-up like a light bulb in a hen house.

Time passed and Gloria was to receive a new mouthpiece, one that would produce low notes more easily on her instrument. The mouthpiece arrived on the day of the concert. Gloria was ecstatic when she found how easily the low notes came on the new equipment.

"The mouthpiece is expensive, so take good care of it," I cautioned her.

That night, as the band waited to go on stage after the orchestra performed, we were lined up against a wall in the hallway and out of sight of the audience. Everyone was anticipating their first concert in the new school, and on an actual stage as well. Gloria was on pins and needles and tried to keep other kids away from her instrument for fear they might accidentally damage her reed. To make sure that didn't happen, she turned the mouthpiece away from the students and toward the wall. She was facing the other way when I said, "Okay, let's go onstage." As she turned back toward the stage she unwittingly rammed the expensive shiny black mouthpiece into the wall, whereupon it shattered into worthless, shiny black (expensive) fragments.

A quick trip to my office to grab the old mouthpiece staved off the shock of losing the new mouthpiece, and we were onstage and ready to go in no time at all. Despite the problem, the concert went just fine and I had a replacement mouthpiece ordered and on its way within a couple of days.

Gloria will probably not remember having to play the instrument with the old mouthpiece, but I don't think she'll ever forget her first Vista concert, or her wonderful shiny gold baritone sax. Gloria turned out to be an exceptional player, and the high school band teacher, Mr. Alvin Carr, was happy to see that she was interested in continuing in band on the baritone saxophone.

Vista survived its early years by the strength of the faculty and its ability to make do under stressful conditions. The open concept went the way of the Edsel in just about three years' time. The principal and teachers from that time frame could tell many stories such as mine; ingenuity and persistence were the modes of the day as we dealt with the problems of change of concept.

CYCLES OF FOURTHS
HARLEY-DAVIDSON
OF TONEVILLE
REPAIR UNIT
HILLTONE
JAZZ
LOUNGE
LOUNGE
Groceries
TONEVILLE TRANSIT
OPERA HOUSE

Snafus and Miscalculations

I refer to the following accounts as Snafus and Miscalculations, as the teacher in the classroom must make choices and often the results can be surprising. In each instance there is a problem and a solution, and the answer to the question, "Was it the right thing to do?" becomes moot.

In addition to solving problems, new construction always seems to create new problems. For example, when the new middle school band room was designed, a sink was to be located at the back of the room. It would be a utility sink for washing instruments. But when construction was completed, the sink, although located correctly, had an unusual feature: the faucet handles were four feet higher than the sink. It seemed that no one could answer the question of its design change, and it looked like I would have to live with it the way it was.

A few days before school opened in the fall, I spotted the architect and builder checking out the building. I asked them both about the handles being located so high above the sink. The architect did not know, but the builder said, "So that you could wash out a sousaphone."

I told him that although it seems to make sense, the fact is that in a middle school it simply won't work. You see, one could stand a student in the sink and turn the faucet on above him or her.

He replied, “They wouldn’t do that, would they?”

I rolled my eyes and said, “Well, of course not.”

He moved the sink handles down that very day.

The next story has a similar ring to it. It is similar only in that the linking element is dealing with the trials and tribulations of new construction. If you have ever remodeled your kitchen and had to fix meals for a week or two in a nearby room, hallway, or garage, you can relate to this experience.

When the new band room construction had been completed at the elementary school, which had been turned into a middle school, I checked out the room. On the wall, about twenty feet apart, were two red fire alarm klaxons—or squawkers, as I call ‘em. I asked why there were two. The architect told me that from his experience as a band student, one squawker likely would not be heard while the band was performing. I told him that it was a middle school band, and a small one at that. He told me to try it out and see how it was when we had a fire alarm. I was leery of that idea but I went along with it.

It was a sunny, fall afternoon and the middle school band was working on a piece of music that was calm and quiet. (Yes, bands can play calm and quiet music.) Suddenly, the two klaxons went off in unison, at about 150 decibels. That is akin to having two jet planes flying ten feet above your house. The students reacted by leaping high out of their chairs, barely hanging on to their instruments as they tried to cover their ears at the same time. For our part, the fire drill was a total disaster. We had terrified kids and dropped instruments, as well as students in tears.

When I gave my report regarding the klaxons, I didn't hold back. I told the architect how traumatizing that experience had been. He apologized and took one of the klaxons out. But the damage had been done. Even with one klaxon working, the sound was still traumatizing to the students. I asked the principal not to schedule fire drills during the band class and he thought that would be a good solution to the problem.

Students make life in band class both fun and interesting, as the students—via their musical abilities together—re-create art by performing music. It sure gets interesting for the band director, who must deal with the students' actions both at school and on field trips, a.k.a. band trips.

On band trips, students were always warned to be on their best behavior, as they represented the entire school while on the trip. Usually, that much warning did the trick, but on one trip I had six or seven students who thought it would be very funny to buy candy cigarettes and root beer in bottles that looked like beer bottles. In all my years of teaching I had never encountered this problem and so I asked them what they were doing.

They all answered so innocently, "We are just having some candy and pop."

I asked them what they thought it looked like while they were doing that and their answer was, "Well it's legal to buy candy cigarettes and root beer, so what's wrong with it?"

Therein lies the mentality of some middle school students. They see themselves differently because they're growing up and they're trying new things to gain attention without breaking rules.

I said, "You actually are breaking rules because you want people to think that you are smoking and drinking. Because of that it would reflect on our school if someone reported the incident to the school. Then you would see that you are in trouble, big trouble." They had not thought of that because it was only candy and pop. I didn't make a big deal out of it by reporting to the principal or the parents, and I think the students appreciated that.

It's not every day, but there are times when the teacher gets stumped and simply can't answer a student's question. All the preparation in college doesn't cover all the answers needed in the classroom, and it can be a challenge to address them all successfully.

For example, a band student came into my office one day, just after band class had started and as the students were warming up their instruments. The student said that his brand-new saxophone played beautifully yesterday but it won't play at all today.

I said, "Oh, it has got to be something small. Let me take a look." I checked all the pads and keys to see if anything might be bent or out of place, but there was nothing that I could find. As a last resort, I decided to look down into the instrument to see if I could find something, but because it was so dark inside I could not see anything. The situation was very disconcerting because I repaired instruments at a music store early in my career, and I was very good at finding and fixing problems with instruments of the band members so that they wouldn't have to take them into town to get fixed. I told the student that I would take the instrument into town myself and bring it back tomorrow.

When I showed the instrument to the repairman, who had worked in the business for over thirty years, I told him that I had checked it out thoroughly from top to bottom and I could find nothing wrong. He asked where the case was and I showed it to him. He glanced inside the case, went back and picked up the saxophone, walked over to his bench, stood the saxophone up, lifted it slightly and suddenly brought it down to the bench top with a sharp rap.

Then came the sound of something falling inside the instrument. We both heard it and he just smiled and said, "That'll be fifty bucks." (He was kidding.) I looked in the bell of the saxophone and there was the mouthpiece cap. Yes, it had been lodged high up inside the instrument and couldn't be seen from above because it blocked the light. The repairman suspected that and checked to see if there was a mouthpiece cap in the case. When he didn't find it, he knew exactly where it was—inside the instrument.

Someone should write a book about these things.

Northern Overexposure

One day in the mid-1990s, I received a phone call at school asking if I was the band director there at Vista Middle School. I assured the caller that I was. He identified himself and asked me if I had any Native Americans students in my band.

I said, "Yes," and he was greatly relieved.

When I asked him what it was all about, he asked me, "How many?" I said that I didn't know right off hand but somewhere in the neighborhood of six.

He asked, "How many in the high school band?" I guessed a total of ten and again asked why he wanted this information. It seemed a bit odd. He said that he was with the television show *Northern Exposure* and that he was charged with casting some Native Americans for an up-coming episode. He told me that I was his last hope. He had called schools from Vancouver, Washington, to the Canadian border and could not find a single school band with actual Native American students playing band instruments in it, until he called me. He also asked me if I was the leader of a Dixieland band called the Bathtub Gin Party Band.

Again I answered, "Yes".

"Well, we need your band, as well, to be in the show." He replied.

I made the effort to gather as many older students as I could, as the gentleman preferred the older high school musicians for the part of a small Native American marching band playing in a parade. I sent out the call and received nine students who wished to do the show for a day's pay of a hundred dollars each. My Dixieland band also received the remuneration, but I was satisfied to be released from school for a day to do the gig and I refused the pay.

The entourage met and rode down to Bellevue together in a charter bus very early in the morning. From there we picked up more personnel and continued on, over Snoqualmie Pass to the town of Roslyn, Washington, four miles northwest of the city of Cle Elum. Roslyn was the make-believe town of Cicely, Alaska, in the television series *Northern Exposure*. The whole town—one main street consisting of two city blocks—was shut down for the weekly filming. The town and the area had special interest for me, as I was returning to the very towns in which I began my teaching career. Since I hadn't seen the area for over thirty years, I was interested in seeing the changes that had taken place.

Arriving on the site, our group exited the bus into a frigid cold that made everyone glad that they had dressed for Alaska. The day was bright. For the participants on that mid-May morning, I warned that the weather in the mountains changes in the afternoon. Sure enough, the temperature had risen to a comfortable sixty degrees by 10:00 a.m. By noon it had risen to eighty degrees. Those "extras" who were to be the crowd at the parade found their parkas had become nearly unbearable. Yet everyone was to stay in costume!

During the morning, the Dixieland band and my students went separate ways as we were in different marching units, but we were all subject to acquiring makeup. The three makeup artists were busy getting everyone looking good for the annual Cicely Parade of the Dead, which borrowed from the traditional Mexican event wherein people celebrate the past by honoring their dead in a ghoulish parade complete with skeletons, ghosts, and other Halloween favorites. I put my makeup on next to the star of the show in the next chair. He was going over his lines as makeup was being applied. Some of our students ate lunch with Ed, one of the Native American characters in the show.

Our students were wearing way too many clothes as the temperature climbed to eighty-plus degrees by shooting time. The crowd, in their parkas, were in bad shape as well. Everyone stayed out of the sun as best they could, but the parade lineup called for everyone to stay put.

It was far worse than any parade lineup I had experienced with my school marching band. The participants had no chance to get out of the sun over the two hours of filming the parade sequence. Water was served constantly but servers couldn't keep up with the demand.

When the parade finally rolled, we circled around the town and went through again and then we were finished. The time was nearly four in the afternoon when we boarded the bus to go home. There were a lot of sweaty bodies on that bus. Comparing sunburns became the activity of choice as we left town.

Now you might not think that the experience was all that educational, but you would be mistaken. As the students themselves said, it was hard work going through the whole day on set but it was worth it. First, it was my opportunity to videotape the whole process from start to finish to show my classes when I returned. Second, the students were said to have been exceptional in their parts. Third, the whole experience culminated in a broadcast television show in which my Dixieland band was only seen on screen for a matter of a few seconds but the students were much more prominently displayed, to my delight.

After the show aired, I received a few thank you notes from parents for involving their kids in the project. Somewhere I have a video copy of the show. I'll save it for my children and grandchildren to watch. The make-believe town of Cicely is a thing of the past, but some of us have the tee shirts that prove it existed—if even for just one day.

GOOD TUNES
N650 1027

The Beat Goes On

When marching season came around one year, the Custer band was eager and ready to go, even though all the pieces of the musical puzzle called a marching band weren't quite in place yet. For example, while we had a sufficient number of most of the instruments covered, the position of bass drummer was not. It seemed like nobody wanted to play the bass drum that year. I even stressed the fact that the whole band depended on the beat of that single drum to keep in step, stay in rhythm, and give strength and stability to the band's performance. They didn't buy it.

Days went by with no bass drummer. It didn't take long before the band felt the absence, but still no takers. That is, until one day a rather bold, young lady decided that she would give up the snare drum and play the bass drum in the parade, since it was pretty evident that something needed to be done for the good of the band.

"The choice of drums will be up to you," I told her, as there were two to choose from. One, a Scotch bass drum, was a tad smaller vertically but a whole lot smaller horizontally. The other choice was the concert bass drum and it was not meant for parade use at all. She chose the big drum despite my warnings of being weighed down like a soccer mom's shopping cart at Costco.

After a while, the idea of the drum being too heavy simply dissolved as the young lady played the drum with all the needed style and vigor that I could ask for in a drummer.

As the Custer band practiced marching from the school eastward and over the freeway overpass, the drummers' favorite thing was to play quietly going up to the bridge and then playing as loudly as possible to watch the cows in the nearby fields bolt and run for the barn. We were the terror of the pasture lands.

One day, while marching on the other side of the overpass, a student from the school came with a message stating that our bass drummer was needed back at the school. Her father had shown up to take her to a doctor's appointment and she was instructed to drop what she was doing and get back to school. She laid down the bass drum and beat it (pun, sorry). Meanwhile, I asked if there was a volunteer who would take the position of bass drummer for a day. I got two responses. Both were from trumpet players who were also brothers. So naturally, I had to wait until the two brothers settled on just who would take the job first. Since the usual way (fighting it out) was not about to happen on my watch, I simply selected one. Both of the boys were large and were prominent members of both the wrestling and the football teams. I felt that the strong beat I wanted was going to be in good hands with these two.

Once the drummers got the "sub" outfitted with the appropriate regalia (drum strap and drumstick) and pointed him in the general direction of march, they gave him the final bit of musical advice. "Just whack that sucker!"

And whack he did. But after marching only a half block down the street I heard an extra *boom*! and a *thud*! and "Ouch!" The bass drummer couldn't handle the weight of the drum and fell forward over the top. Fortunately, he was not hurt, but he didn't want to play that drum anymore. His brother stepped up to the task and donned the drum strap while making utterances about his wimpy brother. He pounded the drum and said, "Let's Go!" He lasted about the same distance as his brother. The band was without a bass drummer for the rest of the practice.

When our regular drummer came back the next day, she heard how the two boys had fallen over playing the drum, and she was the most surprised of all. She could not believe the students' stories until I confirmed them.

The bass drum part was never played more loudly after that, and for everybody in the band, even those two young men, the beat was wonderful.

If I Had a Hammer

While working as band director at Vista Middle School in the early 1990s, my schedule had been changed such that I wasn't the jazz band director anymore and they had to bring another fellow in. I still liked to be there when the kids played, however. So, one night I showed up when the kids were to play at the Haynie Grange Hall near the Canadian border. The gentleman that booked the band told us that we would be playing in a matter of a few minutes, so we needed to get set up as quickly as possible.

There was a problem. The drummer had not shown up. The drums were there, but the drummer had not arrived to play them. As I sat in the audience, the jazz band director approached me and asked if I would play the drums.

I said, "Sure." I went forward and sat down at the drums. I looked around and asked, "Where are the sticks?" I was informed that the drummer always brought his own sticks. I protested that I needed sticks to play, but already the announcer up front was beginning to introduce the band. So Mark, the band director, stopped him and told him that the substitute drummer had no sticks. The announcer thought this would be a good joke and asked the audience,

"Does anyone in the crowd happen to have any drumsticks? Their drummer didn't show up and they need drumsticks for their substitute to play."

After a few minutes a man came forward and said, "I haven't got drumsticks, but maybe you could hit the drums with these." He held out a pair of pliers and a screwdriver.

I said, "I'll take it, because I haven't got anything else." So I sat at the drums with the screwdriver and pliers and tried to figure out how I was going to use them. I opened up the pliers and decided to use them for playing the after beat on the snare drum and decided to use the screwdriver to play the cymbal.

A couple of tunes later a fellow came up to me and handed me two wooden-handled spoons from out of the kitchen. He had a look that said, "Now you can really play. These are the real deal." So, I finished the rest of the program playing with wooden spoons. It worked, and we all had a good laugh.

A Wild Ferry Boat Ride

The Vista Middle School Band was returning home from a successful trip to Orcas Island, where it had performed a concert in a school gymnasium for the students of both Orcas High School and Orcas Middle School. We had received a warm reception from the audience both before the concert and afterwards. Our band had played only for the middle school students prior to that day, and although we were a well-known act at their school, the students in our band wondered whether Orcas High students would even applaud for their music. That thought had crossed my mind as well. But after one song, I knew that it would be okay. The kids in the audience were enthusiastic with their applause, right from the start.

The Orcas band director had called me a month before our visit and asked if we would do him a favor when we came to play.

The favor was simply, "Tell your students to look and play their best for me when they come." Fair enough. The idea of doing any less would never cross my mind, although I admit I questioned why we should do that for him. He continued, "I have started a campaign to get money for construction of a new music facility, and I have used your band as a model for what we are working toward. Your students are in nice uniforms, have good music equipment, and have obvious pride in their school.

We're working on all of those things at present. You see, our band room is the gymnasium. We have equipment that likely came over on the Mayflower, and our student body does not have a handsome-looking band in uniforms. Our sports teams have all of that, but music classes are not in the same class as sports. As a result, we never make any progress toward building a music program." His message was clear and so was my task: I needed to go the extra mile on this gig.

Our ferry ride over to the island was as beautiful as ever, and the students were on their best behavior while enjoying the camaraderie with their peers in a new setting. With three busloads of students, I carried a cadre of chaperones equal to the task of taming wild creatures and teaching them good table manners. One of those was my friend and long-time Vista teacher Mrs. Bernice Graves. Wishing to join the fun, she had requested to chaperone the trip after hearing stories about how much fun the students had on the annual band trip to the San Juan Islands.

The ferry ride back from the island was idyllic up to a point. The point was the end of one of the islands we rode next to on our happy little tour. I caught a glance of the water on the far side of the point and it was charcoal in color with white frosting (waves) that indicated storm conditions. I nearly had a heart attack because, as an avid boater, I knew what was coming.

I bolted from my seat and ran to the stairwell leading to the top deck of the old ferry *Klickitat.* A group of band students were hanging out, looking over the bow rail and not aware of the impending doom that awaited them in just a few seconds! I was in time. I yelled, "Get in here now!" Before I reached the end of the sentence the Klickitat rounded the point and the bow of the ferry dove like a duck. A huge wave came over the top rail and washed the students off their feet and backwards to the cabin where I was waiting, holding the door open. A second wave washed some of them past the door and soon the kids were screaming and fighting their way back to the sliding door in four inches of saltwater. After the last of the students was inside, the place was a madhouse. The combination of a linoleum floor and scrambling students caused the lot of them to slide across the floor and crash into the port side of the cabin, which was U-shaped with the doors on the sides and a stairwell on the open end of the U.

Back and forth the boat rocked with the students having the time of their lives slipping around on the deck of the cabin. It was super fun! I think that the kids would have paid money to do it all again.

But the fun was temporary and fear soon overtook the sliders as the boat seemed to be out of control and at the mercy of the sea. Our Vista chaperone, Mrs. Graves, was white as a sheet, scared to death, and clinging to the narrow vertical column next to her chair that ran from the floor to the ceiling. I asked her if she was okay. Her lack of a response spoke volumes. Other problems popped up. The bathrooms were filled with students throwing up their lunches. Many girls were crying as they came out, only to be continually tossed around by the ferry's wave action and not knowing what to do or where to go. I just told them that all they can do is to sit down and hang on until we were in port. The group spread the word in the bathrooms, and soon the kids were all seated and began hanging on to each other. There were no more sliders, just "hangers on."

The *Klickitat* spent a solid half hour in rough water and finally came into port in Anacortes. The water calmed as the boat came into the last five hundred feet. The students were below deck in the buses and very ready to go home. I checked the entire ferry to see if there might be a student who had not heard the call to return to the cars by the announcer. I found one stray—Mrs. Graves. She was still clinging to the post by her chair.

I approached her, touched her arm, and said softly, "Mrs. Graves . . . we need to board the bus now."

Silence.

I was in the middle of a repeat when she said firmly, "I'm . . . not . . . moving . . . until this boat . . . is at the dock." I stood by with her and then escorted her below to the waiting buses.

The following week I expected to get calls from parents or someone regarding the happenings on the band trip, but I received none. In class, students told and retold their accounts of the ferry ride but little about the concert. I brought it up in class, but it was not what they wanted to talk about, so I gave up.

About a month later I received a written thank-you note from the Orcas Island music director who had invited us. It seems that he had invited the school board members to attend our concert performance and were certifiably impressed enough to approve funds for a music addition and a music program as well! His letter was short but full of pride.

The Vista Band had a regular tour to the San Juan Islands each year, playing on a rotating schedule in the schools of Friday Harbor, Lopez Island, and Orcas Island. Accordingly, the next time our band performed at the Orcas Island school, things had changed. First, our band members were all new, as Vista had become a two-year school. Next, the man who had originally invited us to play had died. Furthermore, we played our concert in a new venue. When we loaded into the performance area I noticed the new construction—a new band room, sporting a folding door that transformed the band room into a concert stage facing out into the cafeteria.

All the efforts of the director and our band had paid off for the students of Orcas Island. Their pride was evident and our playing made the experience memorable. I just wish the other director could have been there.

Dude, Where's My Car?

I looked forward to each day of entertaining/educating the students of my music classes. I loved my job. I had hot- and cold-running students, an amazing faculty, and job security. What's not to like?

One quirky thing about my ever-changing schedule of classes was that I was always a traveling teacher. I worked in as many as five buildings one year. My car was my link to the classes, and getting to class on time was sometimes a challenge. In school, a student arriving to class late would receive 1) admonishment from the teacher, for tardiness, 2) chastisement from the hall monitor, for running, and 3) time after school, perhaps, in the detention room. But me? I got a speeding ticket. Okay, only one, and spread over forty years, not such a big deal.

I arrived at Vista Middle School one sunny day, parked in my usual spot, and entered the building to begin my day of fun and merriment right on time. Everything normal. At 10:00 a.m. I exited the building and found it raining cats and dogs. I stepped over a poodle (sorry), jumped in my car, drove all the way out of the parking lot and to the end of the block, turned into the driveway of Skyline Elementary, and parked around the back of the gymnasium. I entered the school through the side door to the music room.

When my Skyline band class was ended, I exited the building out the front door. Upon seeing the clear blue sky, I simply walked to Vista across the lawn adjoining the two schools. I dodged puddles and poodles (sorry, again) as I went.

After band class at Vista (you still awake?), I went out the front door to get in my car, to go to Eagleridge Elementary, and I found an empty parking place where I remembered parking just a few hours earlier. I hastily searched the parking lot, only to confirm my worst fears: my 1967 baby blue station wagon was gone! I immediately informed the principal, alerted the Eagleridge office, and began a second fruitless search of the parking lot accompanied by the principal. She asked me a lot of silly questions, like, "Are you sure you parked here this morning?" and "Who would ever steal an old wreck like that station wagon of yours?"

"Well, I parked it right here, this morning, and now it's gone!" I told her. "I only have a couple gallons of gas in the car, so the robber won't get far." I envisioned the robber driving south and running out of gas on the freeway in my stolen car. That was the only bright spot at that point.

I called the police. I told them that my 1967 baby blue station wagon with a couple gallons of gas was stolen from the parking lot at Vista Middle School. I was talking to Bellingham's 9-1-1 dispatcher, who passed me off to a patrolman. He sounded concerned. And familiar. Anyway, we talked and the search was on.

"Probably an all-points bulletin," I told myself as I hung up the phone.

Word soon came that my car was spotted hiding behind Skyline Elementary.

"I told you the robber couldn't go very far!" I said, feeling both joy and embarrassment.

I called the cops back and explained that somehow my car was transported, probably by unnamed aliens, to the back of the adjacent elementary school. Hearing this, the patrolman broke out in laughter.

I was ready to hang up when he told me, "Storms, I've seen that station wagon. I didn't bother to call it in. Ain't nobody gonna steal that thing." It was Rod Grove, an old classmate of mine from high school.

Well, that made my day. Actually, it was kind of funny. On the last day of school, my fellow teachers gave me an award for the biggest blunder of the year.

Winner Takes All the Ribbons

In 1993, while on a trip with my professional Dixieland band to our sister city, Myoshi-mura, Japan, I learned a game called Jon-Ken-Pong. It's a game we know as Rock-Paper-Scissors. In the United States, the game is played a bit differently and is one of those games we pick up in elementary school. In Japan, I believe it is much the same. But on the night our entourage learned the game, it was played by a large crowd of mostly adults.

To play the game, one must have a colored ribbon around one's neck. Once the game begins, the ribbon is won or lost to an opponent. The winner takes the loser's ribbon and seeks another player who also has two ribbons and immediately begins another challenge. The game continues until two players have such a collection of ribbons around their necks that it becomes quite a sight. The final pair have a playoff for all the ribbons. The winner is cheered and expected to bow a lot.

When I returned from the trip, I went to the store and purchased five colors of ribbon and set off making ribbon necklaces for use in my elementary music class in Ferndale, Washington. You see, it was a perfect fit: our singing class at Mountain View Elementary had the song "Jon-Ken-Pong" right there in our songbooks. I had seen it there but had always chosen

"Sakura" (Cherry Blossoms), for our Japanese song, since it is so revered in Japan. So the song was new to me as well.

The class enjoyed playing and singing this Japanese game. They were into the third game playoff when a late-arriving student was wheeled into the classroom. The young girl had muscular dystrophy and could only move her hands a little. She appeared happy all the time, with a sweet smile for everyone. I immediately began thinking about how to involve her in the game when the students took over that responsibility. The kids draped her neck with a ribbon and explained the game to her. And then the little darlings cheated! They passed the word around the class to let her win. When she won, the class cheered and gave her all the ribbons. I have never seen a child so happy in all my life. Tears were trickling down her cheeks as the students cheered her.

I came home from that class and related the episode to my wife.

"I only wish that I had a video camera set up to capture that moment," I said.

Whereupon my wife said, "Why don't you do it again and videotape it? I'm sure the kids will go along. In fact, I'll tape it for you. I'd like to see this for myself."

Just as before, the children cheated their little hearts out to get the vignette on tape. I expected the little girl to be late again, so I first bawled the students out for cheating, then I said, "This time it won't be cheating because I said so, and I'm the teacher!"

Near the conclusion of the filming, one student said, "Mr. Storms, she's supposed to bow, but she can't."

"Her tears are her bow," I told her.

Well, things went exactly as planned, tears and all, and the students got to see the heart-warming video before I sent it to the elementary school in Japan that my Dixieland band had visited. They all applauded at the finish. The little girl was the star of the show.

Meeting Needs

Well into my career, my teaching days became tempered by a back problem and its insistence on both demanding and limiting of my physical activity. Despite efforts to restrict my lifting, I continued to challenge my back by lifting more weight than my doctor advised. (I'm guessing I'm not alone on that one.) The weekend gigs I played as a band leader required me to schlep my own sound system to every gig. And since my sound system was a little over ten years old, I considered downsizing to a model that would be just as useful but half as heavy to carry. Only problem was, I had no money for that solution.

The doctor encouraged me to go lighter as soon as possible to avoid more back problems. "You need to lift no more than fifteen pounds," he said.

As a teacher, I rarely missed a day of school. When I was hospitalized for my eventual back surgery I was like a fish out of water. I couldn't wait to get back where I belonged: with the middle school kids, working on music in the classroom, teaching the bands and choir.

When I eventually returned to the classroom and things got back to normal, I noticed that my voice was wearing out by the end of each day. My morning classes were spent mostly working with large music groups, and it soon became apparent that something had to be done about my voice problem, so I sought medical help.

The doctor told me, "You need to speak softer in morning classes. It will go away in a couple of weeks' time."

Most people would celebrate such a simple answer because it didn't cost anything and it would be highly effective, according to the doctor. But for me it was as if someone had told me, "You need to retire." Having spent many years in the same place, doing the same job that I loved, I was pretty shaken by the doctor's advice.

My band room was built for 120 students. In those days, I had 110 students filling those chairs every school day. When a teacher spoke in a moderate tone, the students at the middle and rear of the band couldn't hear. This was easily solved by the teacher speaking twice as loud. It had worked and I had become used to it.

So the needs of weight restrictions, money restrictions, and vocal restrictions were all on my mind as I went to work each day. They were daily issues that needed to be dealt with as I taught classes. I found that I couldn't communicate effectively and couldn't help set up for a concert without careful forethought.

After school on Tuesday afternoons, I hurried to Ferndale High School to work with a new student group I had formed. The players called themselves the Guitar Ensemble. The ensemble was made up of select, outstanding musicians who could play guitars and sing folk songs and light rock tunes that were popular at that time. The leader of this group was a multi-talented boy named Jim Delassio. Besides being a strong leader, he could handle the microphone like a pro. The group had been performing all year and had gained the Ferndale students' respect and admiration. They were popular and I was their proud advisor.

After the group graduated from FHS, some of the ensemble members who had stayed in the area formed a band and played gigs in Bellingham and around Whatcom County. In fact, I received a call from Jim Delassio early on a Saturday evening inviting me to attend his band's opening night at The Vault in Bellingham.

I showed up. Jim Delassio did not. Jim had died in the shower from a grand mal seizure as he was getting ready for the engagement that night. Nothing could have prepared me for this. Although I knew about Jim's epilepsy, but I had no idea it could be fatal.

A few weeks later I received a phone call from Jim's mother. She explained that she would like me to have all of Jim's band equipment, from guitars, amplifiers, and drums, to a rather new sound system. My response was immediate.

"Yes! of course! The Ferndale students will gladly use Jim's equipment. Thank you, thank you!"

I arranged for the guitars to go to the high school, along with the drums, but the sound system was too small for their use. I considered storing it at Vista Middle School, where I taught, but I realized that my personal sound system, although heavier to carry, was better. Again, I stopped to consider the situation. The sound system could stay in one place at Vista.

The answer to my question was answered when I contemplated storing the equipment versus actually using a sound system in the classroom. Nobody did that in those days, on a daily basis, that I knew.

So, I brought my large sound system to school and took the smaller one home. In moving the speakers to my car, I realized that they were half as heavy as the other set and that made me happy because I realized it had solved the problem of me carrying a sound system to gigs with my professional band, Variety.

In class, the new addition of a sound system that allowed the teacher to speak in conversational tones rather than the usual over-the-top volume level was greeted warmly by the band. (Note: In today's classrooms, wireless microphones are used extensively. My sound system is still in use at Vista Middle School, decades later.)

The heartbreaking loss of our beloved Jim Delassio was followed by the joy of using Jim's equipment for decades. The equipment provided joy both for the students and for me—who perhaps gained more than anyone, because that sound system kept me from thinking about imminent retirement. My needs were met.

Thanks, Jim, from each of us. You were a blessing to all.

Guitar Class for All Student

Another year, another schedule change. Although it didn't happen that often, my schedule had flipped midyear, leaving me only two hours of daily classes. I had three bands of only forty minutes each, and when those classes ended I needed something else to fill up my afternoons.

My first idea was to visit other band classes taught by some of the excellent music teachers in our county. For my first trip, I ventured to Lynden to observe Holly Bertran, a good friend and a wonderful teacher.

On my drive to Lynden I saw smoke coming from the back of a house. At first I thought it was simply a trash burn, but then I saw a man in his sixties casually pulling some material from the back of a station wagon that sported a raging fire under the hood and front seat. I pulled in across from his car and ran to help.

He was ever so careful, not in a hurry. I asked if I could help, and I grabbed some of the contents (Watkins Products) and threw them on the grass without breaking them, as fast as I could. The whole thing was emptied very quickly. We stood back, across the street by my car, and waited for the fire engine to arrive. The man said the reason he couldn't work fast was that he had a heart condition and it could be more of a problem than losing the products. The Fire Department soon came and put out the blaze. It was time to move on.

My clothes were bound to smell of smoke, so I explained my helper status to the teacher and his class as soon as I could. The classroom visit was excellent. I watched and learned how another teacher taught the same class with the same beginning band materials that I used. The class visit idea worked so well that I did it about once or twice a week for a few weeks.

Meanwhile, I became bored doing band-library updating and cataloging when I wasn't out gallivanting around the county. I needed a class to teach. With that in mind, I went to the main office to speak to the principal about the matter. As I entered, the science teacher was arguing with the principal about his schedule. It seemed there were too many students in the science rotation, so he couldn't provide enough equipment for the growing number of students. As the teacher was leaving, I stopped him and tried to cool him off by telling him that I might be able to help.

In short order the two of us set up for a guitar class to be part of the Science rotation. I told him that the guitar was the most popular instrument in the United States, and I could capitalize on that interest by teaching a whole lot of students how to play the guitar. After I had secured the change in the class schedule with the science teacher, I was all set. Except for one thing — I didn't know how to play the guitar.

They say that timing is everything. Just before the guitar classes began, I attended the state convention of the Washington Music Educators Association and had the good fortune of locating a man of immeasurable help. His name was Mel Bay. He was the famous Mel Bay, the one who wrote the music book my father used when he was learning to play the mandolin in 1920. Mel Bay was in his early 90s, a small man with great talent and a big heart. He gave me a single guitar lesson and drew up the plan for my class.

"You don't need my books," he said. Just follow my instructions and the students will love the class."

So when students walked into my band room on the first day of the new quarter, they wondered aloud why they were there. It became a happy group of kids when they heard they would learn to play the guitar rather than attend another science class. That class would be made up later in the science teacher's plan, I assured them.

I used a student from the high school to assist me that first quarter. He demonstrated whatever I told him to demonstrate, and we worked Mel's lesson plan like the A-Team. The difference was that bullets didn't fly and there were fewer explosions.

I learned to play the guitar right along with the students and was on my own after the first quarter ended. Because the incoming students had heard good reports about the guitar class from their friends, the class became a joy.

At Christmas break, a student asked if he could take a guitar home for the holidays. I gave the boy permission to do so. They were district-owned instruments, and I made him promise to treat the guitar with care and to be sure to return it.

When the student returned to the class after the break, guitar in hand, he approached me excitedly, saying, "Hey, Mr. Storms! I'm a musician!"

"How did that come about?" I asked.

He told me that no one in his family had ever played an instrument. He added, "When my dad heard me singing and playing those Christmas songs we learned in class, he said, 'Tommy! You're a musician!'"

Talk about seeing joy on a student's face! That kid was a two-hundred-watt lightbulb in jeans.

As the quarter progressed, it seemed everyone was finding joy and success in the guitar classes. The science teacher was happy, too. Mel Bay was right. I kind of missed my ventures out and about; however, the new class was so full of promise that I soon forgot all about going out to gather ideas. I was kept busy applying new ones, for my students, right there at the middle school.

Playing My Way Out of the Hospital

Following a knee surgery, I was bored with life in a hospital bed. I asked my wife, Betty, to bring my flute over to the hospital. She doubted that the staff would permit my playing the thing, but she brought it anyway.

Although hospitalized, I still had my music students in mind. Who would cover my classes? An actual music teacher? Not likely, but it could happen. The usual protocol was to bring in the next sub in line, no matter their specialty. That was what worried me. Anyway, I had to get it off my mind. Hey, I was a patient at the time, not a teacher.

"The flute won't be a problem," I said. "I'll play quietly and keep the door closed." And since I had nobody in the bed next to mine, I knew I could keep it agreeable.

My repertoire was kept on a list in my flute case, for when I played songs for the kids in the elementary music classes. It was mostly classical themes and famous songs that most people knew.

When I had played for about ten minutes, I noticed the door open. I expected someone to enter and talk to me about my intrusion on their hospital stay, but nobody came in.

I got out of bed, hobbled to the door, and closed it quietly. I made it back to bed and began playing the flute once more. Softer though, this time.

Well, that door popped open again, all by itself, and I wondered who was opening it. I left it open that time and played on for about fifteen minutes, until the nurse came in with medication and water on a tray. She said nothing about my flute playing. That is, until she was leaving.

"Please stay in bed and leave the door ajar," she said. "The other patients have enjoyed the music, so I have been trying to let them hear it. Someone has been closing the door. Could that be you?"

"Yes," I said. "I felt I might be too loud if I played regularly."

She said, "Well then, get back to playing regularly." And she left.

After a while of playing symphonic themes, I switched to popular songs, like "Exodus," "The Way We Were," and "Stranger on the Shore." The door opened and again the nurse came. This time she handed me a piece of paper with some writing on it that certainly didn't look medical. It was a list of songs she had gathered from patients within earshot of my room. She asked me to play them.

I laughed and told her that of course I'd play them. I was flattered to be asked.

I counted eighteen songs on the list. Hey, I had the time, so why not?

Food arrived, people came to visit, and soon it was time to think about sleeping. "I can play those tunes tomorrow," I murmured aloud, and went to sleep.

After breakfast I began going down the list, playing song after song until I had most of them played.

Then I received a nice surprise. I was to be released early from the hospital. I called Betty and told her the good news. Within ten minutes she was in the room with me, gathering my things while I sat and watched.

Then I told her about the flute music and the patients' request list. "I guess I won't get to play the rest of those tunes for the folks after all," I said.

But the nurse interjected. "Oh no," she said, "I'm not signing you out until you finish playing the rest of the songs you promised to play. Otherwise, I'm the one who will have to go back and tell each one that you won't be playing their song."

Although she sounded serious I assumed she was joking. Betty was in disbelief but she realized the nurse was serious. So I took my flute and the list and soon earned my release from the hospital by playing the flute to fulfill every request.

"The weird thing was that I never actually saw the other patients or spoke to them," I told Betty on the way home. "The nurse was more than nice, though. She was thankful, too. She had told me that some of those requests were hers."

I wondered if they all were.

BUSINESSES, FLUTES, GUITARS & MORE!

Tightening the Belt

In the middle of the school year, I was summoned to the office to meet with the principal about changing my schedule. The semester was nearly up and I had to deal with all three hundred report cards of my middle school music students, so my time was valuable. It was a Friday.

It seemed there was to be a reshuffling of schedules because the new administration was tightening the financial belt of the school district. By redistributing classes and changing schedules they could eliminate a teacher and, thereby, save money. After I had heard this I wasn't expecting anything unusual. I have been teaching the same subjects for many years. I had three bands, a choir, and a general music class at the middle school. After lunch I had two elementary bands, on alternating days, in other buildings. Changing my schedule did not seem to me like something I should be worried about, so I didn't worry.

When I entered the principal's office she closed the door, which signaled no one else was to hear. The principal started by saying that the administration was going to be shifting things around and I would be teaching a singing class in the elementary school next door, two days a week. I asked her about the situation regarding the classroom, as I was teaching band in that room just prior to the new elementary singing class and there was no music equipment in the room for the students.

"These are second graders who are just learning to read," she said, "so you don't need books." Knowing that there wasn't a piano in that room, just chairs and music stands, I asked her what I should do in the class to educate the students.

"Is there a curriculum?"

"No," she said, "just sing some songs with the kids for half an hour, two days a week, and have fun. They'll love it. They love to sing!"

"Let's see," I figured, "No books, no instruments, no curriculum, and no piano. Looks like I need to dust off my guitar and brush up on my chords to make this work."

I realized what I was getting into but I couldn't quite accept the new gig without asking if this will lead to more elementary classes and fewer classes at the middle school.

"Don't worry about that," she said. "I'm sure the schedule won't stay this way for long."

"Okay, when do I start?"

"Monday," she said enthusiastically.

After band class on Monday, I asked the band students to move the stands out of the way so that my new class could sit in their chairs. That went well and they left. The second-grade class passed them in the hall on their way in.

I introduced myself and the information about music class, and they all clapped their hands. All, except one boy who stood at the back of the room, not seated as he was asked. I asked him to come and sit down with the class, but he refused. I asked him why, and the second grader unloaded a string of expletives worthy of an army drill sergeant. The little darling simply did not want to sing. At this point the words of the principal came back to me: "They love to sing!"

Since it was my first day, I simply asked the boy to sit down at the back of the room and wait until class was over. He didn't have to sing. When the teacher came to pick up her class, I just told her the little boy had said some bad words and refused to participate. She asked me what the words were and I refused to tell her, mainly because her students were right there listening.

Wednesday, when the students came again, first one in the room was the little boy who had caused the problem on Monday. He handed me a note of apology that I could barely read and promised to be good. He said, "I'll be good because my mom said so!"

The singing class went well after that. I didn't even mind when they added two more first grade classes the following year. I had fun teaching those little guys and looked forward to their classes every time because, hey, the principal was right. They really loved to sing.

Fun Day at the Parade

This story is about marching in the Armed Forces Day (or Armistices Day) parade with my high school band in the fall of 1955. The band was marching up Pacific Avenue, the main drag of Bremerton, when we heard jet planes preparing for a flyover. Whenever parades are held in the Navy town of Bremerton, flyovers are scheduled.

During this flyover, we could hear engines of the jets coming closer and closer, up ahead of us, as we marched uphill. As they got closer, the sound got louder and louder, until the sound of those jet planes just sapped the strength from our bodies. One by one or more, we slowly fell to the ground. The bass drummer was the first to go. I was playing the baritone saxophone, which is about a fifteen-pound instrument, and I was probably the next to go. After that, the rest of the band fell to the ground. The parade went into complete chaos. People screamed, even after the flyover. They had flown so close to the buildings that the roar of the four jet planes simply threw the parade into panic. Kids screamed, parents yelled. It was unbelievable.

I remember seeing a news photographer taking pictures of the band lying on the ground. Later, a picture was published in the local newspaper of a man standing on top of a building, standing directly under the jets, holding his hands over his ears.

The photo had been taken from the street level. The four planes, in a diamond pattern, had been approximately fifty feet above the buildings. The law required a minimum of two hundred feet. Heads certainly rolled after that flyover, with the photographic evidence of the infraction published in the newspaper.

Moments after the flyover, the band put itself back together and marched up the street. We heard the jets going away, so we knew things would get back to normal, which they did, pretty much. Toward the end of the parade, about a block from our buses, the sound of the jet planes returned. There came an order to double the cadence. Stricken with fear, the band began to run down the street for the shelter of the buses, before the planes came again. We didn't make it, but we were close. No one fell to the ground that time, but there was panic and screaming by the band students. It was quite an experience. I don't think they pay band teachers enough for those kinds of parades—yet that didn't stop me from becoming a music teacher.

Well, we got on the bus and had quite an emotional bus ride home. We certainly learned something that day: if sound is loud enough, it can sap your strength away.

The Role of the Band

Every band member, of every band, can likely attest to the value and worth of the organization to which they currently or previously belonged. But do they have a concept of the importance the band holds in school and community? The next few stories will explore this subject.

While I attended junior college in Bremerton in 1956–57, our band director, Phil Ager, was asked by the football coach, Dick Ottly, if the band would consent to play for an upcoming championship play-off game. Since the band had never played at any of the prior games, it was a rather special request. After some negotiating, the coach finally struck a deal with the band director that went like this: the band would play for the football game only if the coach required every player on his team to join the choir the next quarter. The reader should know, Phil Ager was also the choir director. At the time, there was only a women's choir.

Ottly countered, "If it's a men's choir, I'll do it."

Perhaps you can envision the scene when, after the championship game was played and won, the players came into the music room the next quarter for the first day of men's choir. There were huge men everywhere, looking as though they were tricked into the situation. They reluctantly sat down. Director Phil told them that because of the deal made they were to not only show up for class but also attend and perform in a couple of concerts. That went over like telling the men's hockey team they were to wear miniskirts and roller skates on the ice.

Within one or two weeks, the athletes began to respond and soon became happy with the class. By the end of the quarter they were ecstatic. And amazingly good. The unusual transformation of athletes to musicians happened because of a need. The need for the band to help the teams win their game was felt strongly enough by the football coach that he bartered his players into the choir for a quarter.

Another instance of this is the amazing Ferndale Golden Eagles' football team. The team played in a play-off game against Prosser High School in 2005. As the Golden Eagles' Band did their usual thing, supporting the team with peppy music, I began to think about the importance of the band and its assisting role to sports teams. So much is taken for granted by most people in this regard. That is, the students in the band are somehow partially responsible for the success of the sports team they play for, just as cheerleaders are, in their role. Oh, and the Ferndale football team won the game *and* the state championship that day. It was a very big deal for the small town of Ferndale to win that championship. The topper is that the band went on to win the state marching band championship that year, as well. I thought it fitting that both the band and the football team shared the spotlight in the town parade that celebrated efforts, skills, and successes.

Just as the coaches and band directors can work together to achieve surprising results, it is interesting to note that after a while the football men in the previous story, the ones forced into the junior college choir, eventually bragged about their men's choir as much as they did their football team!

As a longtime musician, I can attest to the fact that the Olympic Junior College Men's Chorus of 1957 was the best of any junior college men's choirs around the state. The fact that there were likely no others doesn't matter.

ANY TIME
AMADEUS
BIRD
WOOD STOCK
THE MOVIE
WALL ST JOURNAL
DOWN BEAT
DEAF

The Ranger Review - Spring 1957

One of the best things about spring was the annual talent show at Olympic Junior College in Bremerton. The Ranger Review, as it was called, was fun and very entertaining. The event was usually held in the Coontz Junior High School auditorium, which sported a full stage for the show's many and varied acts.

I played baritone saxophone in the Olympic Junior College Dance Band, and we played the show in 1957. Things were going just great, with acts like solo vocalists, instrumentalists, comedians, and even some skits performed on the stage directly in front of our eighteen-piece band that mostly played between acts.

Near the end of the show, while the band performed a number in which the saxophones were featured, something very unusual happened. Something so potentially awful that it might have been tragic on a grand scale. Something really, really scary.

A rope broke high above the performing band members, and that allowed a twenty-foot steel pipe, some three inches in diameter, that was used for holding up scenery, to fall. Right in the middle of the band. (It took four people to carry that pipe off the stage afterwards.) It must have weighed one or two hundred pounds, and it landed neatly between the saxophone and the trombone sections with a resounding *boom!* that sent everyone leaping out of their seats by six inches or more.

For the saxes, who had all been sitting forward on the front of their chairs, it was good that they had been in such good performance posture—the falling pipe tore off the backs of all their chairs. The trombones weren't playing at the time, so no slides were bent. But Terry Strong, the first trombone player, lost the tip of his right shoe. His right foot had been ahead of his left, and the shoe tip had overhung the riser he was sitting on, just enough to get sheared off. How he missed injury is a mystery.

The show came to a dramatic stop, of course. But after a while it began again, this time with no interruptions or falling objects. The school and its auditorium is gone now, yet the memory of that near catastrophe during the Ranger Review of 1957 will remain forever.

A Musician's Nightmare

The phone rang just five minutes before the start of a Seattle Mariners baseball game I was waiting to watch. An important game, this one. The caller was my friend Barry Ulman, who sounded stressed as he asked me if I was busy that night. I told him, "No, I'm just in for another frustrating night of watching Mariner baseball. Why?"

He said, "Great. I need someone to fill in for me tonight. Would you cover the gig for me?" Barry told me that he had fallen a few hours ago and found it impossible to play his instrument.

"Well, in that case, of course I'll play. Which band will I be playing in?"

He replied "It's not a band."

"Not a band? Well what is it?" I asked.

"It's an orchestra, the Skagit Valley Symphony, and the concert is tonight. I have called every clarinet player in town."

At this point, I realized why the lack of available clarinetists was so dire. Barry was in two symphony orchestras, playing second chair in the Whatcom Symphony and principal in the Skagit Symphony. The first parts would be quite exposed, often in the form of a solo or two, during the length of a symphony concert.

Since I had told him that I was not only available but willing to play, I had nowhere to go with this in terms of backing out. "When's the concert and where?" I asked as I checked my watch.

"Seven o'clock at McIntyre Hall in Mount Vernon," he said.

"When's the rehearsal?"

"They're rehearsing as we speak."

This didn't add up to a pleasurable evening of subbing, and it seemed impossible for me even to get there before the gig started, let alone to actually play the gig itself. Yikes! Sight reading the first clarinet part in a symphony concert? Who, in their right mind would actually volunteer to do that?

"I'll pay you seventy-five bucks," Barry pleaded.

"How do I get to McIntyre Hall?" I asked.

"Okay then, get into your tux, pick up the music at my place, and get down there as fast as you can," he said. After that I received the directions to McIntyre Hall and started looking for my tuxedo.

Soon after the mad dash to Bellingham, a mere ten minutes away by cruise missile, I was on Barry's porch accepting the music through his front door. "Good luck!" he said. The forty-minute drive to Mount Vernon ate up more precious time that could have been used to look over the music before the concert. The directions were clear and before I knew it I was parking in the rear lot of McIntyre Hall.

As I approached the hall, I saw a group of men wearing tuxedos at the stage door and heard one say, "Hey, he must be the clarinet player. He's got a clarinet case!" They rushed to greet me.

Wow, these guys sure appreciate their substitute players, I thought. As we entered the rear door and walked down the hall the guys thanked me and patted me on the back for filling in for Barry.

"Have you met the conductor?" said one.

"No," I replied.

"Well, here he comes, I'll introduce you."

"Let's go into a warm-up room," the conductor said after greeting me. I followed him into a small dressing room where he closed the door and said, "Have you seen the music?"

"No" I said, as I put my clarinet together.

The conductor opened the black music folder and removed the program from inside. Without comment he showed me the cover, which sported a nearly full page picture of Barry Ulman with his clarinet.

I stopped putting my clarinet together.

The conductor took out the music for the concert and selected one piece from the lot.

"In the final piece of this concert, you will be featured playing solo clarinet on the *Afro-American Symphony* by William Grant Still. I'm sure you'll do fine." And almost before taking the next breath, he looked at his watch and said, "We're on in ten minutes." He left as I was still holding my clarinet and in a state of shock. I opened the music and found a four-movement symphony with no markings as to solo parts. It looked playable—by a well-rehearsed musician, that is.

Almost as soon as I got my instrument together and was playing the most obvious difficult parts, the door opened and I was besieged with musicians wishing me luck. I wanted to make a break for the door and run for my life, but a young man in the group said, "Mr. Storms, we're all so thankful that you are here to play the part. Do you remember me?" He was one of my students from middle school back when I was a teacher at Vista Middle School in Ferndale.

"Just great," I thought. "I'm about to abandon ship when this kid comes in and tells me how much it means to him and the orchestra. Now I can't leave by that small window."

After shooing them all out, I went back to the music and was nearly able to get through one line when there was a rapping on the door and a voice saying, "On stage in five minutes!" That meant I had only four minutes to either practice or escape. I chose to practice.

The orchestra was soon seated on stage and looked altogether comfortable and relaxed. Meanwhile, I was hurriedly reading the music for the rest of the concert. I turned to the assistant principal clarinetist (second chair) and asked him if he would cover some of the first clarinet solos in the concert so that I could concentrate and study the final piece on the program featuring me on the clarinet. He declined.

As the conductor came on stage to firm applause, he took the microphone and explained to the audience what had happened to Barry and that I would, indeed, be sight-reading the solo clarinet part for the featured *Afro-American Symphony*. Sympathetic yet enthusiastic applause ensued.

The concert progressed and I used the lengthy rests in the music to further my study of the various movements of the solo piece. I had instructed the second chair guy to count the measures for me so that I could get a few more glimpses at the project that awaited me at the end of the concert. He agreed to that request and did a good job of nudging me prior to an upcoming part. I was amazed at how many other solos I had to play in the concert, besides the feature number.

At intermission, I sought a place to study. I returned to my dressing room and was again interrupted by the remaining cadre of instrumentalists that had wished me good luck before the concert.

Again I looked for a door or a window for escape. But I eventually turned again to the music and tried to understand the solo parts. It would have been so much easier if the solos had been marked as such, but they were not. Intermission flew by. So did the second part of the concert, right up to the *Afro-American Symphony*.

Now, I must tell you that, in all honesty, my sight-reading skills are not equal to my technical skills. Knowing this, I had worked on my reading skills over the years by attending the annual Birch Bay Band Workshop, which sight-reads music all week long for six hours a day.

I asked myself why, if I could sight-read music at the workshop every year, should I be afraid of doing that now? Okay, besides the fact that, with this gig, there's also an audience and potentially a total loss of reputation on the line.

The first movement went well. I began to get the feel of the music, which was kind of jazzy in style. I responded by playing the notes in a jazz style and getting into it musically.

By the time the fourth movement was nearly over, I started feeling victorious. I could see the end of the piece and it wasn't technically challenging. I was going to make it! And I didn't mess up a single solo spot, as well. I enjoyed the music as I played and gave in to the piece as a musical experience rather than just a heck of a challenge.

At the conclusion of the *Afro-American Symphony*, the audience gave the orchestra a standing ovation and pointed to me for three standing recognitions. Each time I sat down, the cheers would increase until I stood again.

Needless to say, it was a personal highlight for me, musically.

As I drove back to Bellingham to return the music, I thought about the situation. I had just had a wonderful experience, complete with accolades galore. Barry's accolades. How could I tell him what a grand night it was for me, when it was supposed to be Barry's grand night, the one he had been practicing for the last few months?

When Barry opened the door he sheepishly asked, "How'd it go?"

"Pretty well," I said. "At least nobody threw anything at me." He was smiling and thanking me as we parted.

Back at home, I turned on the television to see how the Mariners did in their game that night. Surprise! They had won! I went to bed a happy man.

SIGHT-
SCREAMING
SCHOOL

From Record to Stage in Fifty Years

I was in the seventh grade, twelve years old, and learning to play the clarinet a little better each day, working on songs from records that my older half-brother, Bud, gave me when he went into the service. There was a stack of music albums by Benny Goodman and Artie Shaw, many of which contained solos that I had memorized note for note by working over them daily in the three years since Bud had left. I worked on albums by other famous bandleaders, too, memorizing the clarinet solos on each of the recordings.

One day I remembered a piece called "Clarinet Polka" that Bud used to play. I didn't have the music, or a recording, but I had heard Bud play it a few times. A friend told me that they played "Clarinet Polka" out at Pearl Maur's Dance Hall on Saturday nights, so I talked to my dad about it and it turned out that he knew Pearl. Dad talked to Pearl on the phone and Pearl told him that I should come out to the dance hall sometime and he would make me a copy of the music. I left immediately.

It was pouring rain outside, but I didn't waste any time. I got on my bicycle and started riding the two miles to the dance hall. It was getting dark when I left. Pearl was there when I arrived, but he had not been expecting me so soon, and by bicycle at that. He was in the middle of doing other things, but he put them all aside so that he could write "Clarinet Polka" for me. I watched him write it from a distance. I was wringing wet.

I had never actually seen music manuscript being written before, so I was watching him very closely. When he finished, he told me that I could not ride home with the music in my hands because the ink would run. We had to put it into something, so he gave me a knapsack.

I got home and began practicing the music immediately. I had only earlier that year learned to read notes, so it was not easy. But it wasn't as hard as learning songs off the records, because I knew how it sounded before starting the project.

I have had a lot of fun playing that polka over the years, mainly for my band students and private clarinet students.

One day in 1999, I got a call to play solo with a concert band, and they wanted me to play, of all things, "Clarinet Polka." I was 62 years old. During that concert, I also played a piece titled "Tribute to Artie Shaw." I had practiced Artie Shaw's music from a record when I was a child. Lo and behold, I am featured fifty years later as a soloist playing Artie Shaw's music and the "Clarinet Polka." As they say in France, *voilà*!

Four concerts were scheduled. I was paid a hundred dollars per concert to perform the two selections.

On the first night, as I waited in the wings and was about to be introduced, my knees began to shake uncontrollably. I walked around. When I performed, my knees began to shake again and it was all I could do to stand still and play. I played the music without incident, thanks to answered prayer and nothing less.

The next two concerts went better. I tried to convinced myself that the light shining on me as I performed was only the friendly spotlight of the yacht club, where I had played for so many years. It worked!

The final performance was on the stage of Mount Baker Theatre, a much larger and more imposing venue. Again, my knees began to shake and weaken, but I kept moving. If I hadn't, I think I would have fallen into a quivering heap of sweat and *clarinetalia*—if that's a word! So, I kind of swayed around, thinking that it might look better than having my knees visibly shaking before the audience. The songs again went well and I soon found myself surrounded with a cadre of well-wishers bearing flowers. Of course, they were the same flowers I had received the last three nights, but this time I could bring them home.

In 2006 I was asked to play "Tribute to Artie Shaw" with the Ferndale High School Band in the end-of-year district band concert. All the district's school bands performed, and again the clarinet solo number came off without a hitch.

All in all, it was quite an experience. One that started me on a few solo appearances with other concert bands, playing—what else—the music of Artie Shaw and "Clarinet Polka."

After all, I have practiced the music for the concerts since I was twelve years old!

Acknowledgements

The work of taking on a book project this late in my life was made much easier by friends and relatives who stepped right in to help. Not surprisingly, they were all teachers too. Many thanks to the folks who made this book what it is: my wife, Marit Aldrich; sister-in-law, Barbara Storms; longtime friend, Bob Kennicott; and graphic artist, Mark Kelly. I am grateful for their assistance in preparing and finalizing this book.

The wonderful drawings were created by my good friend, Mark Kelly, a very talented musician as well as an amazing artist. The illustrations are from Mark's 1988–1989 calendar, *A Day in Toneville,* created for Western Washington University in Bellingham, Washington.

I've enjoyed working on this book, as it allowed me to revisit some favorite moments of my forty-year teaching career. I do miss it. To all my students, and for all the music, many thanks.

LL
U.S.
· MARCELS ·
CONTRABASS SAXOPHONE
MOVING CO.
RHYTHM C

About the Author

Robert "Bob" Storms lives in Ferndale, Washington, with his wife, Marit Aldrich. He has seven grown children, all living in Western Washington. Bob served as a music teacher in the public schools for forty years. He taught band, jazz band, and chorus at the middle school level and general music at the elementary level. In 2000, Bob's peers elected him Outstanding Music Educator of the Year for the San Juan region of Washington Music Educators Association, a state unit of the Music Education

National Conference. Subsequently, he was admitted to the Northwest Bandmasters Association, an organization with an elite membership of outstanding music teachers in the Northwest.

Bob has won three composition contests and authored twelve books of music (1,200 songs in copyright, currently) and numerous pieces for concert band, orchestra, choir, and small instrumental ensembles. *School Stories* is his first book but not his first work of writing. Bob wrote a monthly column for a jazz newspaper, the *West Coast Rag*, for three years in the late 1980s, as well as a weekly column for the *Ferndale Record Journal* in later years.

Now retired, Bob devotes time to composing, writing, guest conducting, guest solo performing, and most of all, playing jazz professionally.